# *Offray* *Glorious* WEDDINGS

Traditions, Inspirations, and Handmade Ribbon Treasures

**ELLIE JOOS**

Photography by George Ross

**FRIEDMAN/FAIRFAX**
PUBLISHERS

**A FRIEDMAN/FAIRFAX BOOK**

©1998 by Michael Friedman Publishing Group, Inc.

Library of Congress Cataloging-in-Publication data available on request

ISBN 1-56799-650-7


Editors: Francine Hornberger and Reka Simonsen
Art Director: Jeff Batzli
Designer: Lynne Yeamans
Photography Director: Christopher C. Bain
Production Manager: Ingrid Neimanis-McNamara
Photography: ©George Ross
Styling: Karin Strom
Photograph on page 136 ©H. Armstrong Roberts

Color separations by Radstock Repro
Printed in England by Butler & Tanner Ltd.

10 9 8 7 6 5 4 3 2 1

For bulk purchases and special sales, please contact:
Friedman/Fairfax Publishers
Attention: Sales Department
15 West 26th Street
New York, New York 10010
212/685-6610   FAX 212/685-1307

Visit our website:
http://www.metrobooks.com

# ACKNOWLEDGMENTS

It is with great appreciation that I thank the talented individuals whose contributions made this beautiful book possible. First, a big thank you to my friends at Michael Friedman Publishing Group for challenging me to create a sequel to *Offray: The Splendor of Ribbon*, especially Francine Hornberger, my fabulous editor, and Chris Bain, who directed the glorious photography. Without their continued support and guidance, this project would have been impossible.

It was a great pleasure working with the following designers who interpreted my visions of the projects in the elegant Offray ribbons that we selected for use in this book. After many years of being in the ribbon business, the relationships with fellow creators is very rewarding and I truly enjoy seeing the results of the creative process. Thank you, thank you, to Doris Coniglio, Phyllis Dobbs, Catherine Horton, Nancy Keller, Dale Nicholson, Marinda Stewart, Laverne Hall, and Patricia Zarak.

Thank you to my dear friend, Karin Strom, whose eye for detail found just the right locations to make the book come alive. We had the good fortune to "invade" the homes of Betsy Schweppe, Gregg Munoz, and Robert Sabo, the lovely Painted Lady in Belvedere, New Jersey, the elegant Rudolfo Ristorante in Gladstone, New Jersey, and the sweetest church, Knowlton Presbyterian in Knowlton, New Jersey. Props and accessories make a big difference between a boring photo and a spectacular photo. I sincerely thank Caroles in Chester, New Jersey, for some of the props used and my talented friend, Ricki Arno of Rosie's Creations, for her breathtakingly beautiful wedding cake and delightful painted almonds. Thank you to George Ross, "photographer extraordinaire," and his energetic assistants. In doing the research for this book, I had the good fortune to spend several hours with Kaethe Kliot in her incredible store, Lacis, in Berkeley, California. What a treasure she and her store are, and I thank her for her valuable time.

It is with great love and gratitude that I thank my family and my dear Bill for their continuing love and support.

And last but certainly not least, a big bouquet of thanks to Claude V. Offray, Jr., and my fellow employees for designing and manufacturing "the world's most beautiful ribbons." For over 120 years, the Offray Company has produced and distributed ribbons for every occasion, including the ribbons that have graced the necks of Olympic athletes, adorned the White House table, and traveled to the stars aboard the space shuttle Columbia. I am extremely proud to be associated with such a fine organization.

# CONTENTS

# INTRODUCTION

Recently I had the great pleasure of assisting my son (my only child) and his bride-to-be in their wedding preparations. Because my future daughter-in-law's mother lived out of state, my role as mother of the groom was expanded, to my delight. It included shopping for the bridal gown and attendants' attire, advising on flowers and menus, and, best of all, decorating the tables, making the pew bows, and creating ribbon headpieces for the bride and her attendants. As Vice President for Publicity and Education at C.M. Offray and Son, Inc., I am constantly promoting uses for our exquisite line of ribbons. Now I had an opportunity to use my skills and talents for real, and with love. It was so much fun and so rewarding to select the ribbons that were used for their wedding, knowing that I was helping to personalize their special day. If you have a wedding coming up—whether your own, a close friend's, or your daughter's or granddaughter's—you, too, will want to make it special, to know that there will never be another like it. This book will help you do that, with many ideas for handcrafting a personal wedding.

After the engagement is announced, the preparations begin for a joyous life together. First, the maid of honor and attendants will want to give a bridal shower. "A Shower of Ribbon Treasures" offers ideas for decorating, including a beautiful breakaway centerpiece, a lace umbrella, and favors. "Dressing the Bride" will give you ideas for personalizing your attire. "Going to the Chapel" presents lovely pew bows, corsages, and even a decorated broom for the African-American tradition of "Jumping the Broom." The reception offers many opportunities for adding ribbons to embellish purchased items like the cake knife and server and the bride and groom's champagne glasses. These ideas and more are found in "The Bridal

'Party.'" The last chapter, "Tying the Knot," provides the basic techniques required to create many of these projects. You'll find familiar techniques such as ribbon weaving and making ribbon roses, as well as new techniques for ribbon flowers and ribbon folding. Once you've learned them, I'm sure you will use them again and again.

As you plan your wedding, you know that you will need "Something old . . . something blue. " Perhaps you have wondered about the origins of certain customs and traditions. In doing the research for this book, I learned so much about weddings past and present, about the meaning of tossing rice, for instance, or the origin of wearing a white dress, and so much more. I've included some of this information and have provided a suggested reading list, should you wish to learn more.

Our choice of ribbons reflects the trend for beautiful colors and the mixing of textures that is being seen in fashion and floral design. You'll find ethereal sheers blending with interesting patterned wire-edge ribbons and luscious classic satins. The resource guide at the back of the book also gives pattern-name information for the distinctive ribbons that were used, which should assist you in identifying these ribbons when you shop. If your color theme is different, simply select similar styles of ribbons in other colors. Offray and its affiliate, the Lion Ribbon Company, have so many options from which to choose that you can be assured that your wedding will truly express your own personality and individuality.

From all of us at the Offray Ribbon Company and Michael Friedman Publishing Group, we wish you a very happy wedding!

*—Ellie Joos*

# CHAPTER ONE

# A Shower of Ribbon Treasures

*We never live so intensely as when*

*we love strongly. We never realize*

*ourselves so vividly as when we are*

*in full glow of love for others.*

—Walter Rauschenbusch

There are two popular versions of the story of the first bridal shower. The more common one is that once upon a time a young lady fell in love with a poor Dutch miller. Her father did not think the miller was a suitable match for his daughter and forbade their union, refusing to provide the necessary dowry. Luckily, the young lady's friends came to the rescue and "showered" her with gifts to start her new household. The second story tells of an Englishwoman who suggested to her friends that they get together before the wedding to present their gifts to the bride all at once, so that each individual gift did not seem too small.

Bridal showers have been popular since the turn of the century. Traditionally hosted by the bride's attendants rather than her family, showers can be as elaborate as a restaurant-catered event or as simple as a potluck brunch in someone's home. But however you choose to celebrate it, the traditions of the bridal shower remain the same. Below you will find a list of some of the most important rituals for this occasion, which have been passed down through the ages.

It is believed that everything the bride says as she opens her gifts will also be said by her on her wedding night. Have someone at the shower record her expressions during the opening of the gifts, then read them aloud to the bride and guests.

As the bride opens her gifts, have someone make the ribbons and bows into a decorative "hat" or a wedding rehearsal "bouquet." Use a sturdy paper plate as the foundation. Poke holes in it and thread the ribbons and bows through the holes, tying the ends together on the underside. This "bouquet" may be tossed at the rehearsal to all single ladies and has the same meaning as the real one: whoever catches it will be the next one to get married.

Tradition says that the bride will have one baby for every ribbon that is broken as she unwraps the presents at her shower. For every broken blue ribbon, she will have a boy, and for every broken pink ribbon, she will have a girl.

Tie the ribbons from the gifts in the bride's hair. As the groom later unties them, he is rewarded with a kiss for each one. Or, if the groom is present at the bridal shower, drape several ribbons around his neck to ward off bad luck.

This chapter presents ideas for making the bridal shower a very special and memorable occasion. Favors and delicate little boxes for hiding treats, a breakaway centerpiece, and the all-important umbrella—these wonderful handmade treasures will show the bride how much her friends adore her, and how they wish her joy and happiness in her new life.

*Combine the techniques of ribbon weaving and ribbon-flower making in wedding or bridal shower favors that will be greatly appreciated.*

## RECTANGULAR BOX

### MATERIALS

❖ 1 yd (1m) of 1½-inch-wide (4cm) satin ribbon in yellow (for wrapping box)

❖ Assortment of satin, grosgrain, and wire-edged ribbons in widths of ⅛, ¼, and ⅜ inches (3mm, 6mm, 10mm) in sherbet colors: pink, yellow, light blue, light green (for ribbon weaving)

❖ 1 yd (1m) of ⅜-inch-wide (1cm) grosgrain ribbon in light blue (for box edging)

❖ 1½ yds (1.5m) of ⅝-inch-wide (1.5cm) satin ribbon in yellow (for cabbage rose)

❖ 2½ yds (2.5m) of ⅝-inch-wide (1.5cm) satin ribbon in light green (for leaves and contrast edging)

❖ 3½-by-3-inch rectangular box

❖ White spray paint, optional

❖ Fusible interfacing

❖ Tacky glue

### DIRECTIONS

1. If desired, spray-paint box white; let dry completely.

2. Around edge of box, glue 1½-inch-wide (4cm) yellow satin ribbon, overlapping slightly at back to finish.

3. Following the instructions on page 133, make a 6-by-9-inch (15-by-23cm) rectangle of ribbon weaving, using the assortment of sherbert-colored ribbons. Allow a ¾-to-1-inch (2–2.5cm) excess for covering lid sides. Position finished weaving on lid top, with right side of weaving facing up. Without trimming, glue weaving in place and let dry.

4. Finish lid by gluing sides down, trimming pleat at corner. Add extra glue to prevent fraying. Trim excess close to lid side edge.

5. Glue ⅜-inch (1cm) light blue grosgrain ribbon around edge of lid.

6. Following the instructions on page 129, make a 2-inch (5cm) cabbage rose from ⅝-inch (1.5cm) yellow satin ribbon.

7. For leaves, cut two 9-inch (23cm) lengths of ⅝-inch (1.5cm) green satin ribbon and form into two loops. Crisscross the loops and glue to lid top. Glue the cabbage rose in the center.

8. Finish box bottom by gluing ⅝-inch (1.5cm) green satin ribbon around sides. Centering ⅜-inch (1cm) light blue grosgrain ribbon over green satin ribbon, glue blue ribbon in place around sides.

# ROUND BOX

## MATERIALS

* 1 yd (1m) of 1½-inch-wide (4cm) satin ribbon in yellow (for wrapping box)

* Assortment of satin, grosgrain, and wire-edged ribbons in widths of ⅛, ¼, and ⅜ inches (3mm, 6mm, 10mm) in sherbet colors: pink, yellow, light blue, light green (for ribbon weaving)

* 1 yd (1m) of ⅜-inch-wide (1cm) grosgrain ribbon in light green (for lid and box edging)

* 1.5 yds (1.5m) of ⅝-inch-wide (1.5cm) satin ribbon in light blue (for cabbage rose)

* 1 yd (1m) of ⅝-inch-wide (1.5cm) satin ribbon in light green (for leaves)

* 3-inch (7.5cm) round box

* White spray paint, optional

* Fusible interfacing

* Tacky glue

## DIRECTIONS

1. If desired, spray-paint box white; let dry completely.

2. Around edge of box, glue 1½-inch (4cm) yellow satin ribbon, overlapping slightly at back to finish.

3. Following the instructions on page 133, make a 6-by-9-inch (15-by-23cm) rectangle of ribbon weaving, using the assortment of sherbert-colored ribbons. Allow a ¾-to-1-inch (2–2.5cm) excess for covering lid sides. Position finished weaving on lid top, with right side of weaving facing up. Without trimming, glue weaving in place and let dry.

4. Finish lid by working a section at a time, smoothing and easing excess over lid sides while gluing in place. Trim excess close to lid side edges. Glue ⅜-inch (1cm) light green grosgrain ribbon around lid edge.

5. Following the instructions on page 129, make a 2-inch (5cm) cabbage rose from ⅝-inch (1.5cm) light blue satin ribbon.

6. For leaves, cut three 7-inch (18cm) lengths of ⅝-inch (1.5cm) green satin ribbon and form each into two pointed loops. Crisscross the loops and glue to lid top. Glue the cabbage rose in the center.

7. Finish box bottom by gluing ⅝-inch (1.5cm) light blue satin around bottom edge. Centering ⅜-inch (1cm) light green grosgrain ribbon over blue satin ribbon, glue green ribbon in place around box.

*Memorable candy or potpourri favors are easy to make with clusters of premade ribbon roses, plain miniature boxes, and glue.*

## PINK BOX

### MATERIALS

- ❋ 1 yd (1m) of ⅜-inch-wide (1cm) grosgrain ribbon in green

- ❋ 32 (8 pkgs) premade mini-swirl ribbon roses in pink

- ❋ 1 premade wire-edge ombré rose in white and cream

- ❋ Papier mâché heart-shaped box, 3 to 4 inches (7.5–10cm) across

- ❋ White spray paint, optional

### DIRECTIONS

1. If desired, spray-paint box white; let dry completely.

2. Glue green grosgrain ribbon on box lid sides, placing ribbon along edge and smoothing in fullness where necessary.

3. Place lid on box bottom. Glue green grosgrain ribbon along box sides, directly below box lid.

4. Glue 16 mini-swirl roses around sides of box bottom.

5. Form ombré ribbon rose into a heart shape and glue in center of lid top. Glue remaining mini-swirl roses around ombré rose.

# CREAM-COLORED BOX

## MATERIALS

- ❖ 1 yd (1m) of ⅝-inch-wide (1.5cm) satin ribbon in yellow

- ❖ 16 (4 pkgs) each premade mini-swirl ribbon roses in white and in ivory

- ❖ 20 (2 pkgs) premade small ribbon roses in cream

- ❖ 10 (1 pkg) premade small ribbon roses in white

- ❖ 2 premade ribbon peonies in ivory

- ❖ Papier mâché heart-shaped box, 3 to 4 inches (7.5–10cm) across

- ❖ White spray paint, optional

## DIRECTIONS

1. If desired, spray-paint box white; let dry completely.

2. Glue yellow satin ribbon on box lid sides, placing ribbon along edge and smoothing in fullness where necessary.

3. Place lid on box bottom. Glue yellow satin ribbon along box sides, directly below box lid.

4. Glue 16 mini-swirl roses around box bottom, alternating white and cream roses.

5. Along one lid side, glue two white ribbon roses at the point of the heart shape, then ten cream ribbon roses, then three more white roses at top along the curve of the heart shape. Repeat along the other lid side.

6. On the lid top, glue a ribbon peony at top and bottom. Glue on six white and six cream mini-swirl roses, using photo as a guide. Form the premade ribbon rose into a heart shape and glue in center opening.

*Whatever you may look like, marry a man your own age — as your beauty fades, so will his eyesight.*

*—Phyllis Diller*

*Simple but elegant candy favors are made with simple wire-mesh purses,*
*premade ribbon roses, and pretty bows from wire-edge ribbons.*

## LAVENDER PURSE

### MATERIALS

❖ 2½ yds (2.5m) of ⅜-inch-wide (1cm) wire-edge ribbon in lavender

❖ ¾ yd (69cm) of ⅝-inch-wide (1.5cm) wire-edge ribbon in light green

❖ 2 premade ribbon roses in cream

❖ 2 premade ribbon tulips in cream

❖ 3 premade small ribbon roses in yellow

❖ Small wire mesh bag

❖ Gold spray paint

### DIRECTIONS

1. Spray-paint the mesh bag gold.

2. Following the instructions on page 123, make a six-loop bow with streamers from 2 yards (2m) of the ⅜-inch (1cm) lavender ribbon. Make four streamers from the remaining ½ yard (50cm) of ribbon.

3. Glue streamers to right corner of purse front. Attach bow above streamers.

4. Gather one edge of the ⅝-inch (1.5cm) light green ribbon. Arrange and glue on left side of purse front.

5. Arrange and glue roses and tulips on purse.

*Marriage is the most*
*natural state of man, and the state*
*in which you will find solid happiness.*

— Benjamin Franklin

# Light Green Purse

## MATERIALS

❖ 1½ yds (1.5m) of ⅝-inch-wide (1.5cm) wire-edge sheer novelty ribbon in pink

❖ ½ yd (50cm) of ⅝-inch-wide (1.5cm) wire-edge ribbon in light green

❖ 2 premade large wire-edge ombré roses in pink

❖ 4 premade large ribbon roses in ivory

❖ 4 premade small ribbon roses in ivory

❖ Small wire mesh bag

❖ Silver spray paint

## DIRECTIONS

1. Spray-paint the mesh bag silver.

2. Following the instructions on page 123, make a six-loop bow with streamers from the ⅝-inch (1.5cm) sheer novelty ribbon. Make two streamers from the ⅝-inch (1.5cm) light green ribbon.

3. Glue streamers to left corner of purse front. Attach bow above streamers.

4. Arrange and glue ribbon roses on purses.

# Pink Purse

## MATERIALS

❖ 1½ yds (1.5m) of ⅝-inch-wide (1.5cm) wire-edge sheer novelty ribbon in pink

❖ 1 premade large wire-edge ombré rose in cream

❖ 5 premade small ribbon roses in white

❖ 4 premade large ribbon roses in white

❖ Small wire mesh bag

❖ Silver spray paint

## DIRECTIONS

1. Spray-paint the mesh bag silver.

2. Following the instructions on page 123, make a six-loop bow with streamers from 1¼ yards (1.25m) of ⅝-inch (1.5cm) sheer novelty ribbon. With remaining 9 inches (23cm) of ribbon, create two streamers.

3. Glue streamers to left corner of purse front. Attach bow above streamers.

4. Arrange and glue ribbon roses on purses.

*A lovely ribbon flower bouquet is the center of an arrangement of six decorated miniature flower pots. The pots are placed around the bouquet to make the centerpiece. At the end of the party each guest is given one tiny pot to keep as a memento of this special occasion.*

## CENTERPIECE

### MATERIALS

❖ 3 yds (3m) of 1½-inch-wide (4cm) wire-edge ribbon in lavender

❖ 2 yds (2m) of 1½-inch-wide (4cm) wire-edge ribbon in peach

❖ 4½ yds (4.5m) of 1⅜-inch-wide (3.5cm) sheer merrow-edge wire ribbon in yellow

❖ 4 yds (4m) of 2⅝-inch-wide (6.5cm) sheer plaid merrow-edge wire ribbon in pastel colors

❖ 2½ yds (2.5m) of 1⅜-inch-wide (3.5cm) sheer merrow-edge wire ribbon in aqua

❖ 1 yd (1m) of 1½-inch-wide (4cm) double-face satin ribbon in ivory

❖ 1 purchased dried stand-up bouquet

❖ 8 purchased silk rosebuds

❖ 1 purchased silk hydrangea in green, split into small pieces

### DIRECTIONS

1. Cut 1-yard (1m) lengths from the lavender and peach ribbon and from 2 yards (2m) of the yellow ribbon. Following the instructions on pages 130 and 126, make a combination of folded and pulled roses from each 1-yard (1m) length, and make a folded rose from double-face satin ribbon. Glue into the stand-up bouquet.

2. Add all the silk rosebuds and small pieces of hydrangea, using photo as guide to glue in place.

3. Cut the 2⅝-inch (6.5cm) sheer plaid ribbon in half. Following the instructions on page 123, make two six-loop bows with these 2-yard (2m) lengths. Cut the 1⅜-inch (3.5cm) aqua ribbon and the remaining 2½ yards (2.5m) of yellow ribbon into five streamers each, for a total of ten streamers.

4. Glue bows and streamers below bouquet, using photo as a guide.

# FAVORS

## MATERIALS FOR ONE FAVOR

❖ 1 yd (1m) each of 1½-inch-wide
   (4cm) wire-edge ribbon in sage,
   lavender, and peach

❖ Variety of premade ribbon roses

❖ 16 to 22 silk rosebuds

❖ 3-to-4-inch (7.5–10cm) clay pot

❖ Oasis to fit pot

❖ Glue gun and glue sticks

## DIRECTIONS

1. Glue oasis into clay pot. Glue silk
   rosebuds into oasis.

2. Gather both sides of each ribbon length
   by carefully pulling on wires, forming
   a 10-inch (25cm) final length. Glue
   around pot.

3. Glue premade roses at center of
   gathered ribbons around the pot,
   using photo as a guide.

*A marriage between*

*mature people is not an escape*

*but a commitment*

*shared by two people*

*that becomes part of their*

*commitment to themselves*

*and society.*

— Betty Friedan

# WEDDING SHOWER LACE UMBRELLA

*Trim a lace umbrella with colorful sheer ribbons to coordinate with
the bride's special color theme or the colors of the season.*

## MATERIALS

- ❀ 9 yds (8.5m) of 2⅝-inch-wide (6.5cm) sheer plaid merrow-edge wire ribbon in pastel colors

- ❀ 10½ yds (10m) of 1⅜-inch-wide (3.5cm) sheer merrow-edge wire ribbon in yellow

- ❀ 4½ yds (4.5m) each of ⅛-inch-wide (3mm) double-face satin ribbon in hot pink, yellow, and aqua

- ❀ 20 (7 pkgs) premade ribbon aster flowers in white

- ❀ Lace umbrella

- ❀ Floral wire

- ❀ Craft wire

- ❀ Purchased wire hearts, optional

- ❀ Glue gun and glue sticks

## DIRECTIONS

1. Cut ten 18-inch (50cm) lengths from the 2⅝-inch (6.5cm) sheer plaid ribbon. Form a 3-inch (7.5cm) loop at one end of each length. Using a small piece of floral wire, wrap around loop to secure in place.

2. Glue loops close to one another around the top of the umbrella, allowing tails to hang down.

3. Cut five 18-inch (50cm) lengths from the 1⅜-inch (3.5cm) sheer yellow ribbon. Following the instructions on page 123, form each length into a two-loop bow. Glue bows around top of umbrella, tucking them into the bottom edge of gathered loops.

4. Cut five 12-inch (30.5cm) lengths from each of the three colors of ⅛-inch (3mm) satin ribbon, for a total of fifteen lengths. Separate them into five groups, each containing one of each color. Fold each group in half and twist a piece of craft wire around the center to form a tassel. Tuck into center of flat bows and glue to secure. Trim ends if needed.

5. Gather one edge of the 2⅝-inch (6.5cm) remaining 4 yards (4m) of sheer plaid ribbon. Adjust gathers so that the ribbon fits the lower edge of the umbrella. Join raw edges, forming a ruffle. Glue to underside of umbrella hem.

6. Cut a 3-yard (3m) length from the remaining 1⅜-inch (3.5cm) sheer yellow ribbon. Loosely fold and drape this length around the umbrella on the top side of the hem, just above the ruffle. Glue to secure.

7. Following the instructions on page 123, form ten two-loop bows from the remaining 5 yards (4.5m) of 1⅜-inch (3.5cm) sheer yellow ribbon. Glue the bows upside down—with tails pointing up—at each corner of the frame. Top off each bow with a premade aster.

8. With the remaining ⅛-inch (3mm) ribbons, working with all three colors as one, loop and drape the ribbons around the umbrella. Glue in place to secure. Glue a premade aster to the top of each loop.

9. Glue on wire hearts at bottom point of each spoke and into the pouf at top, if desired.

# CHAPTER TWO

# Dressing the Bride

*Something old,*

*Something new,*

*Something borrowed,*

*Something blue,*

*With a sixpence in your shoe.*

—Ancient nuptial rhyme

I'm sure that Queen Victoria had no idea what a trendsetter she would become when she married her cousin Albert. In addition to getting married for love, she established other traditions that were popular for many years, including wearing a white dress. Before then, brides wore whatever was their best dress at the time. Although the styles have changed through the years, white is still the most popular color for the bride to wear.

This chapter will show you how to make the accessories that go along with the bridal gown, as well as give you a background on the traditions associated with dressing the bride.

*I love thee with a love*

*I seemed to lose*

*With my lost saints —*

*I love thee with the breath,*

*Smiles, tears, of all my life! —*

*and, if God choose,*

*I shall but love thee better after death.*

—Elizabeth Barrett Browning

# VEILS

A part of the bride's attire that has its earliest roots in superstition and a belief in evil spirits, the veil was meant to protect the bride prior to her wedding. In arranged marriages, it hid the bride's face from the groom until after the ceremony. Queen Victoria's veil of handmade lace would cost $100,000 if duplicated today. In the United States, Nellie Custis, granddaughter of Martha Washington, is believed to have started the custom of wearing a veil because her fiancé remarked on her loveliness after seeing her standing behind a lace curtain at a window.

*Married in white, you have chosen right,*

*Married in green, ashamed to be seen,*

*Married in gray, you will go far away,*

*Married in red, you will wish yourself dead.*

*Married in blue, love ever true,*

*Married in yellow, you're ashamed of your fellow,*

*Married in black, you will wish yourself back,*

*Married in pink, of you he'll aye think.*

—Nineteenth-century rhyme

# BOUQUETS

Imagine a bride during medieval times carrying her bouquet of herbs. Garlic, sage, rosemary, chives, and other pungent herbs were clustered together to create a "bouquet" that the bride carried to ward off evil spirits. After the wedding ceremony, the bouquet was burned in the hearth to chase away these spirits and the ashes were tossed to the wind.

Fortunately, for some time now it has been customary to carry bouquets of flowers. The choice of flowers and the type of bouquet has changed with the fashion of the times. Heavy, extravagant displays—sometimes weighing as much as fifteen pounds—were popular until the 1920s. "Love knots" were a prominent part of these bouquets. These ribbon streamers cascaded from the bouquet and were tied into knots; often blossoms were tied to these streamers and were later cut from the bouquet to give to the departing guests. (Directions to make this kind of bouquet with ribbon flowers can be found on page 34.) Because of the slimmer, streamlined fashion silhouette of the 1920s and 1930s, smaller nosegay-type bouquets were popular at that time. These bouquets featured lilies-of-the-valley, camellias, gardenias, and orange blossoms. Due to the scarcity of fresh flowers in wartime, brides of the 1940s carried fabric-flower bouquets. In the 1960s and 1970s, "flower-child" brides were often married outdoors and carried hand-tied bouquets of simple flowers such as daisies. The wedding of Princess Diana and Prince Charles, seen by millions of brides-to-be, ushered in the return to more elaborate and extravagant bouquet designs.

Today's bride has many options available to her, no matter what the time of year and what the price range. When my son was married, his bride carried a traditional bouquet of roses, gardenias, and loops and streamers of sheer wire-edge ribbons to add length and fullness. For her attendants we made mesh "purses" trimmed with ribbon and silk flowers, thus creating something that would last as a memento of the wedding long after the special day was over.

# GARTERS

Very often the garter is the "something blue" accessory from the famous rhyme. In traditional Christian art, blue, associated with the Virgin Mary, is a symbol of modesty. Early garters were blue silk sashes that were tied below the bride's knee to keep away the wandering hands of the groom and his men. After the ceremony, the garter was snatched away by one of the groom's friends and worn for good luck. Today, as with the tossing of the bouquet, single men line up to attempt to catch the garter; the victor then places the garter on the leg of the woman who caught the bouquet.

# WHAT DO FLOWERS MEAN?

| | |
|---|---|
| Bluebell: | *Constancy* |
| Bridal rose: | *Happy love* |
| Chrysanthemum, white: | *Truth* |
| Daisy, white: | *Innocence* |
| Forget-me-not: | *True love* |
| Hyacinth, white: | *Unobtrusive loveliness* |
| Ivy: | *Friendship, Fidelity, Marriage* |
| Jasmine, yellow: | *Grace and elegance* |
| Lemon blossoms: | *Fidelity in love* |
| Lilac, white: | *Youthful innocence* |
| Lily, white: | *Purity and modesty* |
| Lily-of-the-valley: | *Return of happiness* |
| Magnolia, laurel-leafed: | *Dignity* |
| Orange blossoms: | *Bridal festivities, or "Your purity equals your loveliness"* |
| Rose, white: | *"I am worthy of you"* |
| Sunflower, dwarf: | *Adoration* |
| Violet, blue: | *Faithfulness* |

# BOUQUET WITH LOVE KNOTS

*The romance of love knots, a tradition from days gone by, is re-created in yards and yards of ribbons in this modern bouquet. Cut a knot for each departing guest for good luck.*

## MATERIALS

❖ 2¼ yds (2m) of 1½-inch-wide (4cm) double-face satin ribbon in ivory

❖ 3⅜ yds (3m) of ⅞-inch-wide (2cm) double-face satin ribbon in ivory

❖ 10¾ yds (10m) of ⅝-inch-wide (1.5cm) double-face satin ribbon in ivory

❖ 21 yds (20m) of ⅜-inch-wide (1cm) double-face satin ribbon in ivory

❖ 10 large premade silk flowers

❖ 8 small premade buds

❖ 18 premade lilies-of-the-valley

❖ Fine craft wire

❖ 18-gauge floral wire

❖ Green floral tape

## DIRECTIONS

1. Following the instructions on page 123, make a ten-loop bow from the 1½-inch (4cm) ivory ribbon. Make a twelve-loop bow from an 8-foot (2.5m) length of the ⅞-inch (2cm) ivory ribbon. Set bows aside.

2. Cut six 8-inch (20.5cm) lengths from the ⅝-inch (1.5cm) ivory ribbon. Fold each length in half to form a loop. With fine wire, wire two loops together to an 8-inch (20.5cm) length of 18-gauge floral wire. Cover with floral tape. Repeat with remaining ribbon lengths to create three sets of double loops.

3. Cut four 7-foot (2m) lengths from the remaining ⅝-inch (1.5cm) ivory ribbon. Cut nine 7-foot (2m) lengths from the ⅜-inch (1cm) ivory ribbon. Working with all ribbon lengths combined, fold ribbon in half and wire in center with an 8-inch (20.5cm) length of floral wire. Make random knots in all ribbon lengths alternating spacing. Set aside.

4. Wire the silk flowers and the buds to 8-inch (20.5cm) lengths of 18-gauge floral wire. Cover any raw edges with floral tape.

5. Gather all flowers and buds together. Insert lilies-of-the-valley where needed. Insert the loop-wires from step 2 in the center of the bouquet. Add the knotted ribbons from step 3 to lower part of bouquet. Wire together, forming a handle.

6. Wire the two bows from step 1 to the bouquet handle. Cover all wires on the handle by wrapping with the remaining ⅞-inch (2cm) ivory ribbon.

*Make a padded hanger or decorate a purchased one with premade ribbon
roses and ribbon trim to gracefully support the bride's dress.*

## Ivory Hanger with Ribbon Roses

### MATERIALS

✽ 1 yd (1m) of 1-inch-wide (2.5cm) novelty trim in white

✽ 3¾ yd (3.5m) of ⅞-inch-wide (2cm) novelty lace-and-ribbon combo in white

✽ 3 yds (3m) of ⅞-inch-wide (2cm) double-face satin ribbon in ivory, cut in half

✽ 3 yds (3m) of 1½-inch-wide (4cm) wire-edge sheer ribbon in white, cut in half

✽ 12 premade swirl ribbon roses in ivory

✽ Fine wire

✽ Padded hanger in ivory

### DIRECTIONS

1. Glue the 1-inch (2.5cm) white novelty trim along the sides of the padded hanger. Glue the ⅞-inch (2cm) novelty lace and ribbon combo across top of hanger to measure.

2. Spacing evenly, glue the swirl ribbon roses to the sides of the hanger.

3. Cut the remaining length of novelty lace and ribbon combo in half. Following the instructions on page 123, make four-loop bows from each of these two lengths, from the two lengths of ⅞-inch (2cm) ivory satin ribbon, and from the two lengths of 1½-inch (4cm) sheer white ribbon. Wire one of each type of bow together to form two multibows. Wire the bows to the center of the hanger.

*There is no more lovely, friendly
and charming relationship, communion
or company than a good marriage.*

— Martin Luther

# White Hanger with Ribbon Flowers

## MATERIALS

* ⅜ yd (34.5cm) of 5-inch-wide (13cm) dotted tulle in white

* ¾ yd (69cm) of 1½-inch-wide (4cm) wire-edge sheer/satin-edged ribbon in white

* ⅜ yd (34.5cm) of ¼-inch-wide (6mm) satin ribbon in white

* ¾ yd (69cm) of ⅜-inch-wide (1cm) satin ribbon in white

* 2½ yds (2.5m) of ⅝-inch-wide (1.5cm) wire-edge taffeta ribbon in white

* 1 yd (1m) of ⅝-inch-wide (1.5cm) wire-edge taffeta ribbon in mint

* Pearl stamens

* Stem wire

* White floral tape

* Purchased padded hanger

## DIRECTIONS

1. Following the instructions on page 123, make a two-loop bow from the 5-inch (13cm) dotted tulle. Make a two-loop bow with tails from the 1½-inch (4cm) sheer/satin-edged ribbon. Wire the two bows together and attach to the center of the hanger.

2. Make two streamers from the ¼-inch (6mm) satin ribbon and knot ends. Make four streamers from the ⅜-inch (1cm) satin ribbon and cut ends on an angle. Glue to center of bows.

3. Cut fifteen 5-inch (13cm) lengths from the ⅝-inch (1.5cm) white taffeta ribbon. Following the instructions on page 126, make 15 pulled petals from these lengths.

4. Attach pearl stamens to the top of three stems. Wire five petals around each stem. Cover raw edges with floral tape.

5. Cut six 5-inch (13cm) lengths from the ⅝-inch (1.5cm) mint taffeta ribbon. Following the instructions on page 126, make six pulled leaves from these lengths. Wire three leaves onto each of two stems. Cover raw edges with floral tape.

6. Glue the leaf stems and then the flower stems to the center of the bows.

# BRIDAL SLIPPERS

*Don't overlook this important accessory! Ribbon roses and tiny beads make plain shoes look like magic slippers for a magical day.*

## MATERIALS

* ⅝ yd (57.5cm) of 1-inch-wide (2.5cm) ribbon trim in white

* 1⅝ yds (1.5m) of 1¼-inch-wide (3cm) organdy merrow-edge wire ribbon in white

* 8 (2 pkgs) premade swirl ribbon roses in white

* 1 dozen or more glass pebble beads in crystal

* White fabric shoes

* 5-inch (13cm) length of buckram

* Glue gun with needle nozzle and glue sticks

* Needle and thread

## DIRECTIONS

1. Glue the 1-inch (2.5cm) ribbon trim around the edge of the shoe opening, easing and tucking at center to allow ribbon to conform to curve. Tuck ends under at edges.

2. Cut two circles each 2¼ inches (6cm) in diameter from the buckram. Following the instructions on page 129, make two cabbage roses from the 1¼-inch (3cm) white organdy ribbon. Sew six or more pebble beads to each cabbage rose.

3. Glue the cabbage roses to the center of the shoes, using photo as a guide. Glue two swirl ribbon roses to each side of the cabbage roses.

# BRIDAL GLOVES

*Lace gloves combine with ribbon trim and premade ribbon roses to grace the bride's hands during the wedding ceremony. Place a lump of sugar in the glove as Greek brides do to guarantee a sweet marriage.*

## Rose-Trimmed Gloves

### MATERIALS

❊ 8 (2 pkgs) premade swirl ribbon roses in white

❊ 6 (1 pkg) premade small ribbon roses in white

❊ Glass pebble beads in crystal

❊ 1 pair lace gloves

❊ Needle and thread

### DIRECTIONS

1. Arrange four swirl roses in a slight curve on the back of the glove. Stitch in place. Add a small rose at each end and one in the center. Repeat for the other glove.

2. Stitch pebble beads every ¼ inch (6mm) around the rose cluster.

# GLOVES WITH LACE EDGING

## MATERIALS

❖ 12 inches (30.5cm) of ¾-inch-wide (2cm) ribbon-and-lace trim in white

❖ 2 (1 pkg) premade ribbon roses in white

❖ Glass pebble beads in crystal

❖ 1 pair lace gloves

❖ Needle and thread

## DIRECTIONS

1. Turn under ¼ inch (6mm) on each end of the ribbon-and-lace trim. Pin center of trim to top edge of glove, extending lace past edge of glove. Start pinning trim on the back side, leaving 1½-inch (4cm) gap between ends, to allow glove to stretch when putting it on.

2. Stitch trim to glove, stitching pebble beads every ½ inch (1.5cm). Stitch a ribbon rose to front center of glove. Repeat for the other glove.

*My most brilliant achievement*

*was the ability to persuade my wife to marry me.*

— Winston Churchill

*A delicate garter in the bride's favorite color or in the traditional blue completes the wedding day ensemble.*

# WHITE GARTER WITH BLUE ROSES

## MATERIALS

❖ ¾ yd (69cm) of ³⁄₁₆-inch-wide (4mm) feather-edge double-face satin ribbon in blue

❖ ¾ yd (69cm) of ⅜-inch-wide (1cm) feather-edge double-face satin ribbon in blue

❖ 3 (1 pkg) premade swirl ribbon roses in blue

❖ 8 (1 pkg) premade small ribbon roses in blue

❖ Purchased garter

❖ Fine craft wire

❖ Glue gun with needle nozzle and glue sticks

## DIRECTIONS

1. Following the instructions on page 123, make four- or six-loop bows from both feather-edge ribbons. Wire the two bows together. Attach to the garter.

2. Glue the three swirl roses to the top of the bows.

3. Space the eight small roses around the garter and glue in place.

# *White Garter with Pink Roses*

## MATERIALS

- 24 inches (61cm) of 3/4-inch-wide (2cm) ribbon-and-lace trim in white
- 7/8 yd (80cm) of 3/8-inch-wide (1cm) feather-edge double-face satin ribbon in white
- 1/4 yd (23cm) of 1 1/4-inch-wide (3cm) organdy merrow-edge wire ribbon in white
- 24-by-3 3/4-inch (61-by-9.5cm) white satin fabric rectangle
- 6 (2 pkgs) premade swirl ribbon roses in white
- 12 (2 pkgs) premade small ribbon roses in pink
- 120 glass seed beads in white
- 12 inches of 1-inch-wide (2.5cm) elastic
- Needle and thread
- Glue gun with needle nozzle and glue sticks

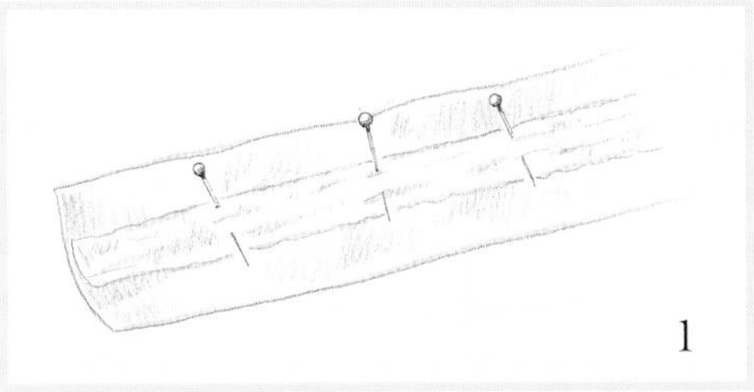
1

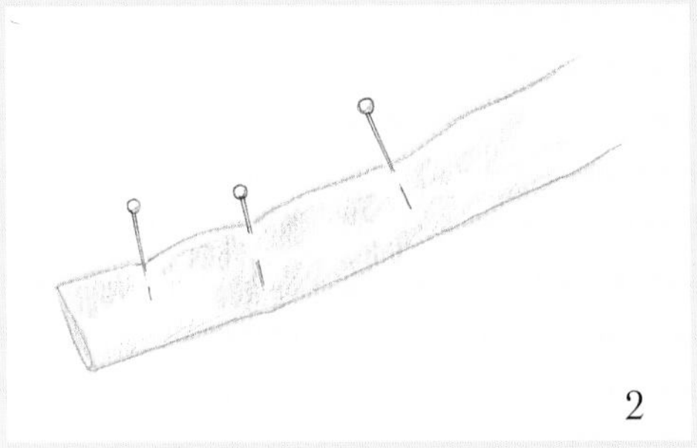
2

## DIRECTIONS

1. Stitch the 3/4-inch (2cm) ribbon-and-lace trim down the center of the satin fabric, on the fabric's right side.
2. With right sides together, fold satin in half lengthwise and stitch edges, starting and stopping 2 inches (5cm) from each end. Turn right side out.
3. With right sides together, pin the two ends together and stitch, forming a tube. Straighten the tube and press the ribbon-and-lace trim to the outside edge of the garter.
4. Insert the elastic and stitch ends together. Whipstitch the opening closed.
5. Cut two 15-inch (38cm) lengths of the 3/8-inch (1cm) white satin ribbon, and knot all ends. Fold ribbons in half, forming four streamers, and glue to center front of garter, using photo as a guide.
6. Fold the 1 1/4-inch (3cm) white organdy ribbon at center to form loops. Wire together. Glue edges of loops on top of streamers on garter.
7. Thread the needle and secure the thread end between the first and second streamers. Thread with 40 white seed beads and go back through fabric 1/4 inch (6mm) from beginning of bead loop. Come back through fabric 1/4 inch (6mm) away and repeat with second loop of 40 beads. Go back through fabric 1/4 inch (6mm) from beginning of loop to secure and make a third loop of 40 beads 1/4 inch (6mm) apart. End 1/4 inch (6mm) from beginning of loop and secure the thread.
8. Glue the six white swirl ribbon roses centered over the streamers. Glue one small pink rose at each end of the swirl rose cluster and one pink rose centered over and under the cluster. Glue two pink roses on each streamer, about 3 inches (7.5cm) apart, alternating spacing on all streamers.

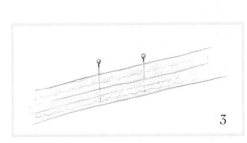

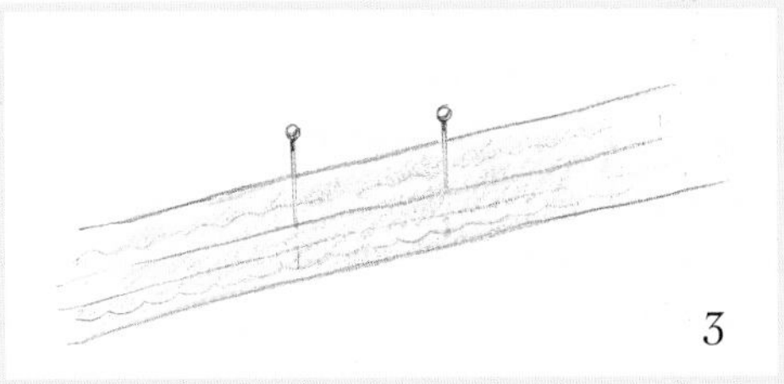
3

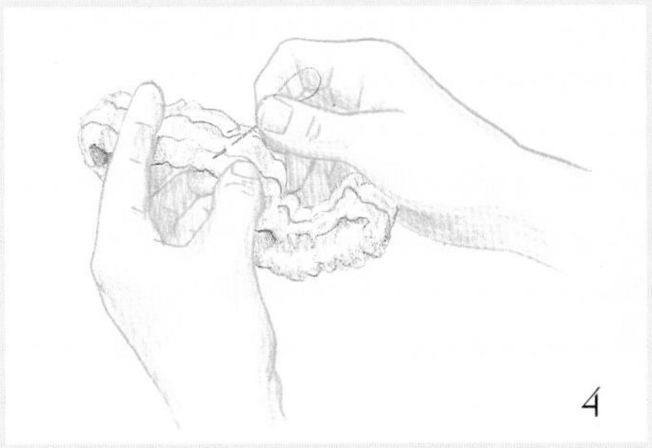
4

## BRIDE'S HEADPIECE

### MATERIALS

❧ 18¾ yds (17m) of 6-inch-wide (15cm) tulle in white

❧ 3¼ yds (3m) of 1½-inch-wide (4cm) wire-edge sheer ribbon in white

❧ 1 yd (1m) of 2⅝-inch-wide (6.5cm) wire-edge sheer print ribbon in white

❧ 4 white satin leaves

❧ 4 pearl loops

❧ Two 3¼-inch-wide barrettes (with removable inner bar)

❧ 28 gauge bead wire

### DIRECTIONS

1. Cut fifteen 1¼-yard lengths from the 6-inch (15cm) tulle. Separate the lengths into five groups of three each. Using one group of tulle streamers, make a 6-inch (15cm) loop at one end of each (leaving 6-inch [15cm] tails). Remove bar from center of barrette to facilitate attaching ribbon loops. Using bead wire, wire loop of tulle streamers to one end of barrette; do not cut wire. Make another 6-inch (15cm) loop and wire this close to the first one. Repeat across top of barrette. With remaining groups of tulle streamers, loop and wire as before to desired fullness. Insert bar back into the center of barrette.

2. Cut two 1-yard lengths from the 1½-inch (4cm) sheer wire ribbon. Take these two lengths and the 2⅝-inch (6.5cm) sheer print ribbons and hold together as one ribbon. Make a 4-inch (10cm) loop at one end of each, (leaving 6-inch [15cm] tails) and wire to other barrette, removing center bar first to facilitate wiring. Make next loop and wire close to first loop across top of barrette. Separate loops to desired fullness. Insert inner bar back into the center of the barrette.

3. Cut the remaining 1½-inch (4cm) sheer white ribbon into four 11-inch (28cm) lengths. Following the instructions on page 130, make a folded rose from each.

4. Wire one rose, one satin leaf, and one pearl loop together in four groupings and glue each across the top of barrette in between the ribbon loops.

# Bridesmaid's Headpiece

## MATERIALS

* 2 yds (2m) of 2⅝-inch-wide (6.5cm) wire-edge sheer printed ribbon in pastel colors

* 1 yd (1m) of 1½-inch-wide (4cm) wire-edge sheer ribbon in pink (or color of your choice)

* 4 satin leaves

* 4 bunches of small silk flowers

* One 3¼-inch-wide (8cm) barrette (with removable inner bar)

## DIRECTIONS

1. Cut the 2⅝-inch (6.5cm) sheer pastel ribbon in half. Take these two lengths and the sheer ribbon and hold as one ribbon. Make a 4-inch (10cm) loop at one end, leaving a 6-inch (15cm) tail and wire to top of barrette close to one end (remove inner bar to facilitate wiring). Make next loop and wire close to first loop. Repeat across top of barrette. Separate loops to create fullness. Insert inner bar.

2. Glue one satin leaf to one bunch of flowers and glue each set to barrette in between ribbon loops.

*Love does not consist in gazing at each other but in looking outward together in the same direction."*

— Antoine de Saint-Exupéry

# FLOWER GIRL'S HEADPIECE

## MATERIALS

* 1 yd (1m) of 1½-inch-wide (4cm) wire-edge sheer ribbon in pink

* 1 yd (1m) of ⅞-inch-wide (2cm) wire-edge sheer ribbon in pink

* 4 satin leaves

* 4 bunches of small silk flowers

* One 2¼-inch-wide (6cm) barrette (with removable inner bar)

## DIRECTIONS

1. Hold the two ribbons together as one. Make a 3-inch (7.5cm) loop at one end, leaving a 5-inch (13cm) tail. Wire to top of barrette at one end, removing inner bar to facilitate wiring. Make next loop with ribbons and wire close to first loop.

2. Repeat across top of barrette. Separate loops to create fullness and reinsert bar into barrette.

3. Glue one satin leaf to one bunch of flowers and glue each set to barrette in between ribbon loops.

*An immature person may achieve*

*great success in a career but never in marriage.*

—Benjamin Spock

# MONEY BAG

*A rectangle of fabric and ribbon flowers are made into a pretty bag to hold the
cards bearing good wishes from the wedding guests.*

## MATERIALS

* 1½ yds (1.5m) of ⅞-inch-wide (2cm) wire-edge ombré ribbon in white and ivory

* ⅞ yd (80cm) of ⅝-inch-wide (1.5cm) wire-edge ribbon in green

* ⅞ yd (80cm) of ⅝-inch-wide (1.5cm) single-face satin ribbon in light pink

* 2 yds (2m) of 1-inch-wide (2.5cm) novelty ribbon trim in white

* 27-by-13-inch (68.5-by-33cm) fabric for bag

* 27-by-13-inch (68.5-by-33cm) fabric for lining

* 2 (1 pkg) premade ribbon roses in ivory

* 8 (2 pkgs) premade swirl ribbon roses in ivory

* 4 (1 pkg) premade ribbon roses in pink

* 6 (1 pkg) premade small ribbon roses in pink

* 3 inches (7.5cm) rattail cord in white

* ¾-inch-wide (2cm) pearl button

* Needle and thread

## DIRECTIONS

**Note**: All seams are ½ inch (1.5cm) unless otherwise stated.

1. With right sides together, fold up one edge of the bag fabric 10½ inches (26.5cm); bag now measures 16½ by 13 inches (42 by 33cm). Stitch side seams, stopping the stitching ½ inch (1.5cm) from top edge. Repeat for lining fabric. Turn right side out and press.

2. Following the instructions on page 129, make two cabbage roses from the ⅞-inch (2cm) ombré ribbon and eight folded leaves from the ⅝-inch (1.5cm) green ribbon.

3. Cut ⅝-inch (1.5cm) light pink satin ribbon into two lengths. Make a small gathered rose from each length by stitching across long edge, pulling tightly, and stitching ends together.

4. Decorate the bag with the ribbon roses and leaves, using photo as a guide. Stitch in place. Stitch a piece of the 1-inch (2.5cm) novelty ribbon trim in place across the flap edge on the right side of the fabric.

5. Fold the rattail in half to form a loop. Stitch at center of bag flap. Stitch remaining length of 1-inch (2.5cm) novelty ribbon trim at side edges to form shoulder strap.

6. With right sides together, pin top and side edges of bag and lining together. Stitch up side, across edge, and down side, being careful not to catch inside of bag, lining, or shoulder strap.

7. Place bag lining inside bag and pin remaining edge of bag and lining together. Stitch across, leaving a 4-inch (10cm) opening for turning. Turn bag right side out and press. Whipstitch opening closed.

8. Fold flap down and mark position for button. Stitch in place through both bag and lining fabric. Make a tiny stitch in each bottom corner through all layers to hold lining in place.

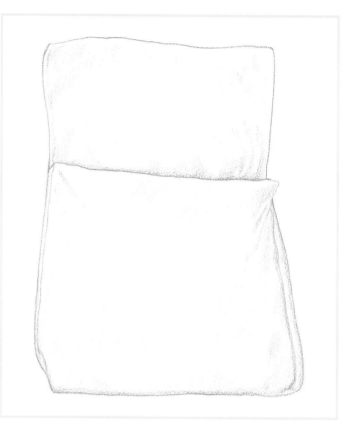

*For a simple yet elegant look, glue ribbon roses of different styles to wide headbands in shades of white and ivory for the bride and pastel colors for the bridesmaids or flower girls.*

## ROSE HEADBAND WITH CREAM AND WHITE ROSES

### MATERIALS

- ❖ 1¼ yds (1m) of ⅝-inch (1.5cm) single-face satin ribbon in white

- ❖ 1 pkg rose garland in white

- ❖ 4 (2 pkgs) premade small ombré roses in white to cream

- ❖ 6 (2 pkgs) premade swirl ribbon roses in cream

- ❖ 7 (2 pkgs) premade swirl ribbon roses in white

- ❖ 4 (2 pkgs) premade ribbon peonies in cream

- ❖ 4 (1 pkg) premade large satin roses in white

- ❖ ¾-inch (2cm) headband

- ❖ Tacky glue or hot glue

### DIRECTIONS

1. Wrap the headband with the ⅝-inch (1.5cm) white satin ribbon. Glue in place. Wrap the headband with the rose garland, making sure roses remain on the right (upper) side.

2. Glue the premade flowers on the headband randomly, using photo as a guide.

# Rose Headband with Pink Roses

## MATERIALS

- ❀ 1¼ yds (1m) of ⅝-inch-wide (1.5cm) single-face satin ribbon in white
- ❀ 14 (5 pkgs) premade ribbon asters in pink
- ❀ 20 (2 pkgs) premade small ribbon roses in rose
- ❀ 9 (3 pkgs) premade sheer ribbon roses in pink
- ❀ ½ yd (50cm) of 1¼-inch-wide (3cm) wire-edge sheer ribbon in pink
- ❀ ¾-inch (2cm) headband
- ❀ Tacky glue or hot glue.

## DIRECTIONS

1. Wrap the headband with the ⅝-inch (1.5cm) white satin ribbon. Glue in place.

2. Glue the ribbon asters and roses on the headband randomly, using photo as a guide.

3. Following the instructions on page 123, make a two-loop bow from the sheer ribbon and attach it to the top of the headband.

*To love someone*

*is to see a miracle*

*invisible to others.*

*—François Mauriac*

# ORANGE BLOSSOM COLLECTION

Herbs and flowers have been an integral part of wedding celebrations for hundreds of years. The orange blossom, a Mediterranean symbol of fertility, is one of the few plants that blossoms and bears fruit at the same time. Actual blossoms dipped in wax were worn in the bride's hair, carried as part of her bouquet, and placed on her dress for happiness and fertility. Queen Victoria's wedding ensemble prominently featured orange blossoms, thus establishing this flower as a fashionable item of the times; the practice lasted until the 1930s. One Victorian ladies' magazine even stated that no "self-respecting" bride would get married without the proper display of orange blossoms as part of the ensemble.

Using buds and blossoms re-created by Lacis owner Kaethe Kliot, together with beautiful ribbons, this lovely collection is perfect for the bride who desires a Victorian-inspired wedding.

The bridal wreath is actually a kit that has been further embellished with calla lilies made from wire-edge ribbons and streamers of feather-edge double-face satin ribbon. The bouquet is made of a variety of buds and blossoms with additional ribbon flowers. To complete the ensemble, the collection includes a simple and elegant boutonniere for the groom. (Available from Lacis—see sources.)

*Queen Victoria on her wedding day.*

*The Bridal Wreath should not be worn after the wedding-day. The bridal wreath, the bridal bouquet, and the orange blossoms from the wedding-cake if treasured as mementoes of the happy event, should be preserved in the recesses of a locked drawer in the bride's chamber, and not exhibited under glass shades in the drawing room.*

—Manners and Rules of Good Society (1886)

*Mamma came before and brought me a Nosegay of orange flowers....I wore a white satin gown with a very deep flounce of Honiton lace, imitation of old. I wore my Turkish diamond necklace and earrings, and Albert's beautiful sapphire brooch.*

—Queen Victoria
From her journal, February 10, 1840

# BOUTONNIERE

## MATERIALS

❉ ¼ yd (23cm) of 2-inch-wide (5cm) wire-edge taffeta ribbon in cream

❉ 1 yd (1m) of ³⁄₁₆-inch-wide (4mm) feather-edge satin ribbon in ivory

❉ 1 orange blossom bud cluster

❉ 2 small ivy leaves

❉ 2-inch (5cm) chenille stem in yellow

❉ 16- or 18-gauge covered floral wire

❉ Green floral tape

❉ Lightweight floral wire

❉ Needle and thread

❉ Corsage pin

## DIRECTIONS

1. Following the instructions on page 132, make one calla lily from the 2-inch (5cm) cream taffeta ribbon and the yellow chenille stem.

2. Secure the orange blossom bud cluster, calla lily, and ivy leaves together with floral tape.

3. Cut the ivory feather-edge satin ribbon into two 18-inch (50cm) lengths. Working with two lengths as one, tie a small bow around clustered flowers to finish.

# BOUQUET

*Fragrant orange blossoms, immortalized by Queen Victoria, were once indispensable to Victorian brides.*
*Here, with beautiful ribbons, they again speak of good fortune and happiness.*

## MATERIALS

* 5⅓ yds (5m) of 1½-inch-wide (4cm) ombré wire-edge taffeta ribbon in white and ivory

* 12 inches (30.5cm) of 2-inch-wide (5cm) wire-edge taffeta ribbon in cream

* 1½ yds (1.5m) of 1½-inch-wide (4cm) chenille-stripe chiffon ribbon in ivory

* 3½ yds (3.5m) of 2¾-inch-wide (7cm) wire-edge floral-print chiffon ribbon in ivory

* 25 small ivy leaves

* 8 large ivy leaves

* 2 orange blossom bud clusters

* 3 orange blossom bud leaf clusters

* 6 small bouquet blossom clusters

* 3 large bouquet blossom clusters

* 9 pearl cluster stamens

* 4-inch (10cm) chenille stem in yellow

* 16- or 18-gauge covered floral wire

* 24-gauge paddle wire

* Green floral tape

* Needle and thread

* Knitting needle or 16-penny nail

* Glue

## DIRECTIONS

1. Following the instructions in chapter five, make individual flowers. From the 1½-inch (4cm) ombré taffeta ribbon, make six trilliums and three orchids. From the 2-inch (5cm) cream taffeta ribbon and the yellow chenille stem, make two calla lilies. Attach two small ivy leaves to each calla lily. Set aside.

2. To assemble the bouquet, cut one 9-inch (23cm) and two 7-inch (18cm) lengths of covered floral wire. In the following steps, attach flowers with paddle wire and cover with green floral tape as needed.

3. Using the 9-inch (23cm) wire as a foundation, start at one end and attach three small ivy leaves. Add one bud leaf blossom cluster. Add a calla lily and ivy pieces to each side of the foundation wire. Next add a trillium and attach a bud leaf blossom to each side. Set foundation unit aside.

4. For each of the two side units, use the 7-inch (18cm) lengths of covered floral wire. Attach two small ivy leaves to the end of the wire. Add one bud cluster and one bud leaf cluster. Next add one trillium. Attach two small ivy leaves and one large ivy leaf to each side of a large blossom cluster and attach this unit to top of 7-inch (18cm) length of covered wire. Repeat for second unit.

5. Attach one side unit to each side of the foundation unit.

6. Attach one large ivy leaf and two small ivy leaves to one bud leaf cluster. Repeat and wire one grouping to each side of bouquet.

7. Attach the three orchids in the center of the bouquet.

8. Following the instructions on page 123, make a four-loop bow from the 1½-inch (4cm) chenille-stripe chiffon ribbon. Attach to base wire above the orchids.

9. Add one large blossom bouquet to the center.

10. Add three trilliums. Attach two large ivy leaves and one small ivy leaf to each side.

11. Following the instructions on page 123, make a four-loop bow with a center loop and 18-inch (50cm) streamers from the 2¾-inch (7cm) floral-print chiffon ribbon. Leave a companion 18-inch (50cm) tail. Attach to the top of the bouquet. Cut all ribbon ends to a V to finish.

# BRIDAL HEADPIECE OR WREATH

## MATERIALS

- ❋ 1 yd (1m) of 2-inch-wide (5cm) wire-edge taffeta ribbon in cream

- ❋ 7 yds (6.5m) of 3⁄16-inch-wide (4mm) feather-edge satin ribbon in ivory

- ❋ Orange Blossom Bridal Wreath Kit

- ❋ 8 small ivy leaves

- ❋ 4 orange blossom buds

- ❋ 12-inch (30.5cm) chenille stem in yellow

- ❋ 16- or 18-gauge covered floral wire

- ❋ Needle and thread

## DIRECTIONS

1. Following the instructions on page 132, make six calla lilies from the 2-inch (6cm) cream taffeta ribbon and the yellow chenille stem, using 6 inches of ribbon per flower.

2. Assemble headpiece as directed in kit. Insert the calla lilies and ivy leaves evenly as shown. Join the ends together to make a circlet.

3. Loosely wrap 3¼ yard (1m) of the feather-edge ribbon around the circlet.

4. Cut 1¼ yards (1m) from the remaining feather-edge ribbon and form four streamers each about 10 to 12 inches (25.5–30.5cm) long. Attach two streamers at each side of circlet. Tie two orange blossom buds to streamers on each side.

5. Cut the remaining feather-edge ribbon in half and make two four-loop bows, following the instructions on page 123. Attach bows above streamers.

6. If desired, cut the comb that comes with the kit in half with wire cutters and attach half to each side of wreath for wearing.

# CHAPTER THREE

# Going to the Chapel

*Love is patient and kind; love is not jealous or boastful; it is not arrogant or rude. Love does not insist on its own way; it is not irritable or resentful; it does not rejoice at wrong, but rejoices in the right. Love bears all things, believes all things, hopes all things, endures all things. Love never ends. . . . So faith, hope, love abide, these three; but the greatest of these is love.*

—I Corinthians 13:4–8,13

The time has arrived for that special moment…the walk down the aisle. You may be escorted on the arm of one or both parents, or a close friend. Attendants will lead the way, and flower girls may toss rose petals from a pretty basket covered with ribbon roses. This custom began in small villages where children would toss petals across the bride's path to prevent the emergence of evil spirits from below.

Your ceremony, whether simply stated or enhanced with your own written vows, will include the exchange of rings, the circular shape representing the eternity of your love. Although today's rings are usually made of gold or platinum, earlier rings were made from a variety of materials such as iron, steel, and even leather. Following are some other wedding traditions you may have been curious about.

It is lucky for the bride and groom to find a horseshoe on their wedding day. It is good luck for the bride to be kissed by a chimney sweep because he is associated with light and warmth. It's lucky to marry on the groom's birthday, but not on the bride's. And it's bad luck to be late for your wedding.

June is a popular month for weddings, for several possible reasons. In Roman mythology, Juno, the queen of the gods, is also the goddess of marriages. The longest day of the year is in June, promising a long and happy life, and June is filled with flowers.

A bride carries a handkerchief to catch her tears. The bride keeps the handkerchief through the years to give to her eldest daughter for good luck on her own wedding day. If it rains on the day of her wedding, the bride will not have to shed tears herself. If the bride looks at the sun when leaving for her wedding, her children will be beautiful.

To guarantee a long and "binding" marriage, the wedding couple should carry a knotted ribbon between them at the ceremony. Also, the bride traditionally stands to the groom's left. This practice dates back to the time of marriage by capture, when the groom needed to leave his right hand free for defense.

Since it was believed that a vein runs directly from the heart to the fourth finger of the left hand, the wedding ring has traditionally been placed there to keep love from escaping from the heart. The wedding ring represents a "circle of love" that has no beginning or end and will last forever. If the groom makes a wish as he puts the ring on the bride's finger, his wish will come true.

In this chapter, you will learn to make the props for the wedding ceremony, from pew bows to the ring bearer's pillow to unity candles symbolizing the union of the two families.

*From the very first God made man*

*and woman to be joined together*

*permanently in marriage; therefore*

*a man is to leave his father and*

*mother; and he and his wife are united*

*so that they are no longer two,*

*but one. And no man may separate*

*what God has joined together.*

*— Mark 10:6-9*

# "FROM SIMPLE TO SUBLIME"
## PEW BOWS

*The charm of pew bows can be created simply with several ribbons in bow combinations, or made more elaborate with the addition of strings of pearls and graceful lengths of tulle flowing from pew to pew.*

## MATERIALS FOR ONE BOW

* 4½ yds (4.5m) of 2⅝-inch-wide (6.5cm) brocade merrow-edge wire ribbon in ivory, plus additional 2 yds (2m), optional, for more elaborate bow

* 4½ yds (4.5m) of 1½-inch-wide (4cm) wire-edge sheer ribbon in ivory

* 1 yd (1m) of 2⅝-inch-wide (6.5cm) wire-edge sheer ribbon in ivory

* 2 yds (2m) of ⅞-inch-wide (2cm) novelty woven ribbon in white, optional, for more elaborate bow

* 2 to 3 branches of ivy

* Pearl strands, optional, for more elaborate bow

* Tacky glue or hot glue

## DIRECTIONS

1. Cut three 1½-yard (1.5m) lengths from the 2⅝-inch (6.5cm) ivory brocade ribbon. With right sides out, make a 6-inch (15cm) loop at one end of each. Wire all three lengths together and notch ends.

2. Following the instructions on page 123, make a twelve-loop bow with 16-inch (40.5cm) tails from the 1½-inch (4cm) ivory sheer ribbon. Wire this bow to the loops from step 1.

3. Following the instructions on page 129, make a fancy pulled rose from the 2⅝-inch (6.5cm) ivory sheer ribbon. Glue the rose to the center of the ribbon bow.

4. Glue the ivy to the pew bow.

5. For a sublime look, follow the instructions on page 123 and make a six-loop bow from the additional 2 yards (2m) of the 2⅝-inch (6.5cm) ivory brocade ribbon. Set aside. Cut a 47-inch (1.2m) length of the ⅞-inch (2cm) white novelty ribbon to make a tail and wire to the back of the twelve-loop bow. Wire together with the six-loop bow and wire all three ribbon loops.

6. For a truly magnificent look, cut four 6-inch (15cm) lengths from the remaining ⅞-inch (2cm) white novelty ribbon. Make ribbon loops, wire together, and glue to sheer bow. Add more ivy to top of bow. Add pearl strands on each side and one in center. The perfect finishing touch is to loosely drape fine tulle from pew to pew. See picture on page 64.

*Fragrant rose petals fill a sweet little basket decorated with sheer wired ribbons and premade ribbon roses. A matching headband completes the look.*

## FLOWER BASKET

### MATERIALS

**Note:** Number of roses required will vary with size of basket.

❀ 2 yds (2m) each of ⅞-inch-wide (2cm) sheer ribbon in white novelty and pink

❀ ½ yd (50cm) fabric remnant, optional

❀ 16 (6 pkgs) premade large white ribbon roses

❀ 20 (5 pkgs) premade wire-edge ombré roses in pink and white

❀ 24 (8 pkgs) premade ribbon asters in white

❀ 1 yd (1m) pearl string

❀ White basket, 7 inches by 9 inches oval across (18 by 23cm) by 5 inches (13cm) high (not including handle)

❀ Glue gun and glue sticks

### DIRECTIONS

1. If desired, cover the inside of the basket with the fabric remnant. Measure basket height and circumference and add 1 inch (2.5cm) to each measurement for seams. Cut a fabric rectangle from these measurements for basket sides. Stitch rectangle together, forming a tube. Trace bottom of basket and add ½ inch (1.5cm) around tube for seams. Attach lower edge of rectangle to stitched tube, forming basket lining. Put inside basket and glue in place.

2. Glue the large white roses around the lower edge of the basket.

3. Glue the ombré roses around the basket sides.

4. Glue the asters along the upper edge of the basket, covering the edges of the lining.

5. Cut the ⅞-inch (2cm) sheer ribbons in half. Following the instructions on page 123, make four six-loop bows from these 1-yard lengths. Cut the pearl string in half, tie one length around the center of each bow, and let hang as streamers. Wire bow to each basket handle.

# Flower Girl's Headband

## MATERIALS

❁ 2 yds (2m) of ⅝-inch-wide (1.5cm) satin ribbon in white

❁ 1 yd (1m) each of ⅞-inch-wide (2cm) sheer ribbon in white novelty and pink

❁ 2½ yds (2.5m) pearl string

❁ 2 (1 pkg) premade large wire-edge ombré roses in pink and white

❁ Child's headband

❁ Batting remnant

❁ Tacky glue or hot glue

## DIRECTIONS

1. Wrap the batting around the headband and glue in place.

2. Wrap the ⅝-inch (1.5cm) white satin ribbon around the headband and glue in place.

3. Glue the pearls around the headband.

4. Following the instructions on page 123, make one four-loop bow with streamers from the ⅞-inch (2cm) sheer ribbon. Tie the remaining pearls around the center of the bow and let hang as streamers. Attach the bow to the center of headband.

5. Glue the ombré roses to the center of the bow.

# JUMPING THE BROOM

In a recent book, author Harriette Cole explains the history of a custom that had its roots in the days of slavery and is still part of many modern African-American wedding ceremonies. At a time when slaves were considered property and not permitted to get married, "Jumping the Broom" was a way for African-American couples to make a statement to their community about their relationship. The broom represented their new life together. The couple would hold hands and jump over the broom, symbolically jumping into their new life. Today, brooms are once again being used to symbolize the beginning of a couple's married life, connecting the couple to their cultural heritage. The brooms are decorated with ribbons in the colors of the wedding theme, as shown on page 75, and may be embellished with cowrie shells, which symbolize fertility and good luck.

# BROOM

*Gold ribbons and cowrie shells decorate a plain straw broom to incorporate cultural traditions into an African-American wedding ceremony.*

## MATERIALS

❖ 18 yds (16.5m) of 1½-inch-wide (4cm) wire-edge metallic ribbon in gold

❖ 12 inches (30.5cm) of 2⅝-inch-wide (6.5cm) organdy merrow-edge wire ribbon in ivory

❖ 2¼ yds (2m) of ⅞-inch-wide (2cm) wire-edge novelty woven ribbon in white and gold

❖ 1¼ yds (1m) of ⅝-inch-wide (1.5cm) wire-edge metallic ribbon in gold

❖ Handful of cowrie shells and/or jewels such as pearls

❖ 36-inch (1m) craft broom

❖ Glue gun and glue sticks

## DIRECTIONS

1. Cut sixteen 20-inch (51cm) lengths from the 1½-inch (4cm) gold metallic ribbon. Following the instructions on page 129, make sixteen pulled roses from these lengths. Set aside.

2. Cut a length from the remaining 1½-inch (4cm) gold metallic ribbon long enough to wrap several times around the broom handle. Secure with glue at the top and bottom of the handle.

3. Gather the 2⅝-inch (6.5cm) ivory organdy ribbon by gently pulling the wire on one edge, being careful not to pull the wire out of the ribbon. Glue around the base of the handle, forming a skirt.

4. Glue three of the pulled roses to the top of the broom handle.

5. Cut the ⅞-inch (2cm) white-and-gold novelty woven ribbon and ⅝-inch (1.5cm) gold metallic ribbon into 20-inch (51cm) lengths. Wrap around a pencil to curl. Glue four lengths under the roses.

6. Glue the remaining thirteen roses above the skirt, all around the broom.

7. Curl the remaining lengths of ribbon. Glue under the skirt all around the broom.

8. Glue several cowrie shells and/or jewels randomly on the broom.

# RING BEARER'S PILLOW

*Take two lace-trimmed hankies and add an array of ribbons and premade ribbon roses to make a cushion to lovingly hold the bride and groom's wedding bands.*

## MATERIALS

- ❖ 3 yds (3m) of ⅞-inch-wide (2cm) gold-merrow-edge wire ribbon in ivory

- ❖ 4 yds (4m) of 1½-inch-wide (4cm) gold-edge sheer ribbon in ivory

- ❖ ½ yd (50cm) of ³⁄₁₆-inch-wide (4mm) feather-edge double-face satin ribbon in white

- ❖ 1 premade large ombré rose in ivory

- ❖ 8 (2 pkgs) premade mini-swirl ribbon roses in ivory

- ❖ 4 (2 pkgs) premade small ombré roses in ivory/white

- ❖ 4 premade ribbon asters in ivory

- ❖ 4 pearl sprays

- ❖ 5 clear pony beads

- ❖ Two 14-inch (36cm) doilies or napkins with lace edge

- ❖ Batting

- ❖ Buckram

- ❖ Needle and thread

- ❖ Glue gun and glue sticks

## DIRECTIONS

1. Place the doilies or napkins with wrong sides together. Stitch together around inner edge of lace, leaving a 4-inch (10cm) opening for stuffing. Stuff with batting, and stitch opening closed.

2. Following the instructions on page 129, make four cabbage roses from the ⅞-inch (2cm) ivory ribbon and the buckram. Set aside.

3. Cut the 1½-inch (4cm) ivory sheer ribbon into 1-yard (1m) lengths. Thread all four lengths through one pony bead. Push bead to center of ribbons. Divide ribbons above bead into two groups of two ribbons each. Thread a pony bead on each group. Repeat for ribbons below bead.

4. Glue the center pony bead in the center of the pillow. Position the remaining four pony beads at the four corners of the pillow. Adjust ribbons as needed and glue beads in place.

5. Glue the four pearl sprays to the center pony bead as shown. Fold the ³⁄₁₆-inch (4mm) white satin ribbon in half and glue center of ribbon to center pony bead. This ribbon will be used to tie the rings onto the pillow. Glue the large ombré rose in the center.

6. Glue a cabbage rose on top of each corner pony bead. Embellish the pillow with the remaining premade flowers, using photo as a guide.

# UNITY CANDLES

*The unity candle ceremony represents the union of the two families. The bride and groom light the individual tapers and bring the two flames together to light the larger column. This is similar to the South African !Kung ceremony in which fire from the hearths of the homes of both families is used to start a fire in the newlyweds' home. Our candles are personalized with the addition of the wedding invitation and sheer wired ribbons.*

## MATERIALS

❖ 1 yd (1m) of ½-inch-wide (1.5cm) woven braid in white

❖ 1½ yds (1.5m) of 1¼-inch-wide (3cm) sheer merrow-edge wire ribbon in white

❖ 1 yd (1m) of 1¼-inch-wide (3cm) sheer merrow-edge wire ribbon in ivory

❖ 1½ yds (1.5m) of 1½-inch-wide (4cm) sheer ribbon in white

❖ 3 (1 pkg) premade ribbon lilies in white

❖ 1 large faceted crystal, ¾-inch (2cm) diameter, with hanger

❖ 2 sets of 3 crystals to string together, 1 long and 2 short per set

❖ 1 white 3-by-10 inch (7.5-by-25cm) pillar candle

❖ 2 white 12-inch (30.5cm) tapers

❖ Wedding invitation

❖ White ball-head pins

❖ Hot glue

❖ Glue release pad

❖ Double-stick tape

❖ Fine craft wire

## DIRECTIONS

1. With a pencil, trace an oval shape around the text of the wedding invitation. *Do not cut.* Working over a glue release pad, place a small amount of glue on the raw end of the woven braid. Let and dry completely, then make a clean cut. Starting with this end, glue the braid to the invitation, placing it over the pencil line. When braid ends meet, repeat same procedure to close braid oval. Let dry. Carefully cut the excess paper away from the braided oval.

2. Affix the invitation to the pillar candle with double-stick tape. Push the white ball-head pins through the braid into the candle, spacing them evenly around the oval.

3. Cut an 18-inch (50cm) length of the 1¼-inch (3cm) sheer white ribbon. Following the instructions on page 123, make a four-loop bow from this length. Cut a 12-inch (30.5cm) length of the 1¼-inch (3cm) sheer ivory ribbon and make a slightly smaller two-loop bow from this length. Wire the ivory bow to the top of the white bow, attaching the large faceted crystal in place while wiring. Glue one of the ribbon lilies in the center of the bow. Pin the bow in place at the bottom of the invitation. Hide the pins behind the bow loops.

4. Cut the 1½-inch (4cm) sheer white ribbon in half. Following the instructions on page 123, make a two-loop bow with 6-inch (15cm) tails from each length. Set aside. With the remaining 1¼-inch (3cm) ivory sheer ribbon, make two additional bows as in step 3. Wire one to the center of each sheer white bow. Wire a set of crystals hanging down at the center of each bow, placing longer crystal in middle. Glue a ribbon lily to the center of each bow. Wire bows to bottom of taper stems or to candlestick bases.

The honor of your presence
is requested at the marriage of
Miss Nadeszhda Archipov
and
Mr. Joseph Charles Fobert III
on Saturday, the fifteenth of July
nineteen hundred and ninety-five
at four-thirty o'clock
Christ Episcopal Church
Budd Lake, New Jersey

*Ribbon roses, wire-edge sheer ribbons, and feather-edge satin ribbons combine in a corsage that makes an elegant addition to the groom's mother's wedding attire.*

# MOTHER-OF-THE-GROOM CORSAGE

## MATERIALS

- ❀ 1⅞ yds (1.75m) of 1½-inch-wide (4cm) wire-edge ribbon in pale yellow

- ❀ 1⅝ yds (1.5m) of 1½-inch-wide (4cm) wire-edge ribbon in pink

- ❀ 2½ yds (2.5m) of ⅞-inch-wide (2cm) wire-edge sheer novelty ribbon in light coral

- ❀ 1½ yds (1.5m) of 3⁄16-inch-wide (4mm) feather-edge satin ribbon in powder pink

- ❀ 1½ yds (1.5m) of ⅜-inch-wide (1cm) feather-edge satin ribbon in powder pink

- ❀ 3 pearl cluster stamens

- ❀ 5 large ivy leaves

- ❀ 4 small ivy leaves

- ❀ 24-gauge floral wire

- ❀ 16- or 18-gauge covered floral wire

- ❀ Green floral tape

- ❀ Knitting needle or 16-penny nail

- ❀ Corsage pins

## DIRECTIONS

1. Cut both the 1½-inch (4cm) yellow and the 1½-inch (4cm) pink ribbon into 5-inch (13cm) lengths. Following the instructions on page 127, make two yellow rolled petal roses and one pink rolled petal rose from these lengths. Make buds from the remaining petals.

2. Following the instructions on page 123, make an eight-loop bow with a small center loop from the ⅞-inch (2cm) sheer coral ribbon. Secure the loops with fine wire. Working with both widths of feather-edge ribbons as one, make a four-loop bow in the same manner.

3. Wire the roses and buds together with the 16- or 18-gauge covered floral wire as shown, adding ivy leaves as needed. Wire the sheer and feather-edge bows together, placing in the center of the corsage.

4. To wear, secure with corsage pins.

# MOTHER-OF-THE-BRIDE CORSAGE

(This corsage is worn draped from the front of the shoulder to the back.)

## MATERIALS

- ❧ 2⅔ yds (2.5m) of 1½-inch-wide (4cm) wire-edge ribbon in lavender

- ❧ 1¼ yds (1m) of 1½-inch-wide (4cm) wire-edge ombré ribbon in white and ivory

- ❧ ½ yd (50cm) of 2-inch-wide (5cm) wire-edge ribbon in cream

- ❧ 1 yd (1m) of 2¾-inch-wide (7cm) wire-edge pastel chiffon ribbon

- ❧ 2 yds (2m) of 1½-inch-wide (4cm) chenille-stripe chiffon ribbon in turquoise

- ❧ 1 yd (1m) each of ³⁄₁₆-inch-wide (4mm) feather-edge satin ribbon in sage green, ivory, and powder pink

- ❧ 20 small ivy leaves

- ❧ 4 large ivy leaves

- ❧ 6 pearl cluster stamens

- ❧ 12-inch (30.5cm) chenille stem in yellow

- ❧ 16- or 18-gauge covered floral wire

- ❧ 24-gauge fine wire

- ❧ Green floral tape

- ❧ Needle and thread

- ❧ Corsage pins

## DIRECTIONS

1. Cut the 1½-inch (4cm) lavender ribbon into three 32-inch (81cm) lengths. Following the instructions on page 132, make three orchids from these lengths. Cut the 1½-inch (4cm) ombré ribbon into three 16-inch (41cm) lengths. Following the instructions on page 131, make three trilliums from these lengths. Cut the 2-inch (5cm) cream ribbon into three 6-inch (15cm) lengths. Following the instructions on page 132, make three calla lilies from these lengths and the yellow chenille stem.

2. To assemble, cut a 9-inch (23cm) length of the covered floral wire. Start at the front end of the corsage and attach a calla lily with two small ivy leaves. Cover the wires with green floral tape as needed. Next add a trillium. Work in ivy leaves as desired. Add an orchid, a calla lily, another orchid, and a trillium. Use the large ivy leaves in the center of the corsage. Continue with an orchid and trillium and finish with a calla lily.

3. Cut the 2¾-inch (7cm) pastel chiffon ribbon into five lengths, approximately 7 inches (18cm) each. Fold each piece into a loop and wrap with wire to secure. Cover with floral tape. Attach throughout corsage as shown.

4. Cut a 1¼-yard (1m) length of the 1½-inch (4cm) turquoise chiffon ribbon. Following the instructions on page 123, make a two-loop bow with 14-inch (36cm) streamers from this length. Fold remainder of ribbon in half and attach to the bow in the middle. Secure loops and tendrils with fine wire. Attach to the center of the corsage.

5. Wire all three lengths of sage, ivory, and pink satin ribbon together at centers. Attach to the center of the corsage; three tendrils should fall to the front and three tendrils to the back. Cut all ribbon ends into a V to finish.

6. To wear corsage, gently curve foundation wire to fit over the shoulder. Secure with corsage pins.

Let all thy joys be
as the month of May,
And all thy days be
as a marriage day....

—Francis Quarles

# WEDDING HEART WREATH

*Create a romantic wreath of ribbons and silk flowers to announce the special event to all in your neighborhood.*

## MATERIALS

❁ 5 yds (4.5m) of 2⅝-inch-wide (6.5cm) wire-edge white brocade ribbon

❁ 3½ yds (3.5m) of 2⅝-inch-wide (6.5cm) wire-edge sheer print ribbon in ivory

❁ 1½ yds (1.5m) of 2⅝-inch-wide (6.5cm) wire-edge sheer print ribbon in white

❁ 2 berry-and-leaf clusters in ivory and gold, each about 24 inches (61cm) long

❁ Heart-shaped twig wreath, about 24 inches (61cm) in diameter

❁ Craft wire

❁ Wire for hanging wreath

## DIRECTIONS

1. Open up the berry-and-leaf clusters. Place one on each side of the wreath and wire into place.

2. Cut a 2⅝-yard (2.5m) length of the 2⅝-inch (6.5cm) white brocade ribbon. Following the instructions on page 123, make a six-loop bow with 12-inch (30.5cm) tails from this length. Cut a 2-yard (2m) length of the 2⅝-inch (6.5cm) sheer ivory print ribbon and make an eight-loop bow from this length. Wire together with the first bow and attach to center of the wreath at the dip of the heart, positioning the tails so they point up, not down.

3. Cut two 22-inch (56cm) lengths of the white brocade ribbon. Following the instructions on page 124, make two "loop and tail" shapes from these lengths. Glue at the top of the wreath in the extension of the center bow, placing tail in similar formation to center bow tails.

4. Cut the 2⅝-inch-wide (6.5cm) sheer white print ribbon in half. Following the instructions on page 124, make two sets of "loop and tail" shapes from each of these lengths. Repeat with the remaining 1½ yards (1.5m) of sheer ivory print ribbon using same lengths. Nestle and glue a pair of ivory and white "loops and tails" onto each side of the wreath, positioning the loops so they fan out and the tails drape down to the point of the heart.

5. Following the instructions on page 123, make a two-loop bow with 8-inch (20.5cm) tails from the remaining white brocade ribbon. Wire the bow at the point of the heart, catching in and adjusting the tail ends so they are under the bow.

6. Trim all tails cleanly and neatly. Attach wire hanger loop to the back of the wreath.

# BRIDE'S GOING-AWAY HAT

*Perfect for an outdoor wedding, this decorated hat features ribbon flowers, bows, and veiling.*

## MATERIALS

- 3½ yds (3.5m) of 2¾-inch-wide (7cm) chiffon print merrow-edge wire ribbon in pink

- ⅔ yd (61cm) of 2-inch-wide (5cm) wire-edge taffeta ribbon in cream

- 4¼ yds (4m) of 1½-inch-wide (4cm) wire-edge ombré ribbon in shades of pink

- 8 small ivy leaves

- 3 pearl cluster stamens

- 24-gauge floral wire

- Glue gun and glue sticks

- Purchased straw hat

- 24 inches (61cm) of ivory hat veiling

## DIRECTIONS

1. Cut a 24-inch (61cm) length of the 2¾-inch (7cm) chiffon print ribbon. Place the 2-inch (5cm) cream taffeta ribbon underneath the chiffon ribbon. Wrap the ribbons around the crown of the hat to make a hatband. Turn under raw edges. Glue to hat.

2. Following the instructions on page 123, make a six-loop bow with a center loop from the remaining chiffon print ribbon. Secure the loops with floral wire. Attach to the center back of the hat, covering the hatband seam.

3. Cut the 1½-inch (4cm) ombré ribbon into three 50-inch (127cm) lengths. Following the instructions on page 128, make three camellias from these lengths. Glue the camellias to the front of the hat. Arrange the ivy leaves among the flowers and glue in place.

4. To attach the veil, tie a small overhand knot at each end of the veil. Glue the knot under the lower edge of the hatband 8 inches (20.5cm) from the center front on each side. Tuck the veil ends under the front lower edge of the hatband to secure. Glue as needed. Adjust veil over the front brim of the hat to partially cover face.

# CHAPTER FOUR

# The Bridal "Party"

Throwing rice, nuts, or fruit at the bridal couple as they leave the ceremony is said to bring them all the good things in life. Today's wedding guests often choose flower petals or birdseed to toss, or soap bubbles to blow, or jungle bells tied together to shake as the couple departs from the church.

The celebration that follows the wedding ceremony is as unique and personal as the couple itself. It is a time to rejoice and enjoy the results of months of planning and preparations. Your personal style has determined the type of celebration it is to be, whether small and intimate with close family and friends or the "party of a lifetime" with a cast of thousands! Long ago, wedding "breakfasts" took place in the church hall. In rural America, it was traditional to be married in the family home with friends and neighbors assisting in the festivities by bringing food. The menu always included the wedding cake, a tradition dating back to the Romans. The barley or wheat cake was an offering to Jupiter. After tasting it, the groom broke it over the bride's head as a symbol of abundance or fertility. Early Britons baked large baskets of crackers for weddings and for the guests to take home.

In the seventeenth century, when Charles II returned to England from exile in France, he brought French chefs with him. These chefs started the custom of tiered cakes by icing stacks of sweet buns with sugar. When the sugar hardened it was topped with toys and figurines.

Today's cakes are often topped with a miniature bride and groom. I especially like the latest trend of decorating wedding cakes with ribbons and ribbon flowers.

In this chapter, there are many ribbon ideas, decorations, and favors to personalize your celebration. If you are traditional, you will toss your bouquet and garter and exit in grand style in a ribbon-embellished wedding car.

*Cherished memories are preserved for years to come in a guest book embellished
with lace appliqués, ribbon roses, and a closure made from a sheer wire-edge ribbon.*

## PENHOLDER

### MATERIALS

❖ ¾ yd (69cm) of ½-inch-wide (1.5cm) novelty trim in white

❖ ⅜ yd (34.5cm) of ⅜-inch-wide (1cm) double-face satin in ivory

❖ 6-by-6-inch (15-by-15cm) fabric remnant in ivory

❖ Variety of ribbon roses in ivory

❖ Batting

❖ Purchased penholder

❖ Glue gun and glue sticks

### DIRECTIONS

1. Glue the batting and fabric remnant to the top of the holder, making a hole for the pen.

2. Glue the white trim around the sides of the holder. Glue the ⅜-inch (1cm) ivory satin ribbon across the corners as shown.

3. Glue the ribbon roses around the pen hole.

# GUEST BOOK

## MATERIALS

* 2½ yds (2.5m) of 1½-inch-wide (4cm) wire-edge sheer novelty ribbon in ivory

* 5 yds (4.5m) of ¾-inch-wide (2cm) novelty trim in white

* ½ yd (50cm) satin fabric remnant in white

* Several packages of premade ribbon roses

* Several lace appliqués

* Tassel

* ¼ yd (23cm) batting

* Purchased guest book with removable pages

* Tacky glue

* Glue gun and glue sticks

## DIRECTIONS

1. Remove the pages from the guest book.

2. Cut two pieces of fabric the exact measurements of the inside of the book covers. Spread the inside front cover with tacky glue and attach one of the cut fabric pieces. Repeat for inside back cover. Let dry.

3. Close the book. Place batting around the outside of the book and cut to fit exactly. Spread cover with tacky glue and attach batting.

4. Cut a piece of fabric the size of the book's outside dimensions plus 1 inch (10cm) all around.

5. With the book open, position fabric on outside and bring around to inside of cover. Glue in place with tacky glue. Check the tension by closing the book several times. Cut away any excess.

6. For the ties, cut two 1-yard (1m) lengths of the 1½-inch (4cm) sheer ivory ribbon and glue one to the inside of each cover. Close the book. Cut the remaining ½-yard (50cm) in half and place these lengths diagonally, side by side, across the upper right corner of the book.

7. Glue the ¾-inch (2cm) white novelty trim around the edges of the inside book covers, covering all raw fabric edges. Glue the remaining novelty trim around the edges of the outside of the book.

8. Glue the lace appliqués, tassel, and ribbon roses to the cover at center and corners, using photo as a guide.

## Ribbon Place Card

### MATERIALS FOR ONE PLACE CARD

❖ 6 inches (15cm) of ¼-inch-wide (6mm) gold merrow-edge wire ribbon in ivory

❖ 1 large ribbon flower in ivory

❖ Place card

❖ Glue gun and glue sticks

### DIRECTIONS

1. Glue the ribbon across the place card. Glue the flower at the left side.

## Rose Place Card with Bow

### MATERIALS FOR ONE PLACE CARD

❖ 6 inches (15cm) of ⅞-inch-wide (2cm) gold-edge sheer ribbon in white

❖ 1 premade small gold rose

❖ Place card

❖ Glue gun and glue sticks

### DIRECTIONS

1. Following the instructions on page 123, make a two-loop bow with the ⅞-inch (2cm) sheer white ribbon. Glue the bow at the left side. Glue the rose in the center of the bow.

# BRIDAL CHAIR BACK SWAG

*Blooming roses and spectacular ribbons designate the bride's chair as the place of honor.*

## MATERIALS

❖ 7 yds (6.5m) of 2⅝-inch-wide (6.5cm) wire-edge sheer ribbon in ivory

❖ 4 yds (4m) of ⅞-inch-wide (2cm) double-face satin ribbon in ivory

❖ 3⅓-inch yds (3m) of 2⅝-inch-wide (6.5cm) wire-edge sheer print ribbon in ivory

❖ 1 yd (1m) of 1½-inch-wide (4cm) double-face satin ribbon in ivory

❖ One 24-inch premade silk flower swag (or wire two 12-inch swags together in the center)

❖ Additional silk or dried roses as desired

## DIRECTIONS

1. Bend swag into half-moon shape to fit chair. Glue or wire additional roses to swag if desired.

2. Cut 2 yards (2m) from wire-edge sheer ivory ribbon and make a six-loop bow. Glue or wire to center of swag. Cut remaining length in half and make two four-loop bows with streamers. Glue or wire bows to each end of swag.

3. Cut l yard from wire-edge sheer print ivory ribbon and make a four-loop bow. Glue or wire to sheer ribbon center bow. Cut remaining length in half and make two three-loop bows with streamers. Glue or wire to sheer ribbon end bows.

4. Cut ⅞-inch-wide (2cm) double-face satin into four lengths. Tie two lengths to each side; one length will hang down and the other length on each side will be used to tie swag to chair.

5. Loosely drape and glue 1½-inch-wide (4cm) double-face satin ribbon into swag.

THE BRIDESMAIDS

# BIRDCAGE ENVELOPE HOLDER

*A gilded cage decorated with silk hydrangeas and spectacular floral sheer wired ribbons is a lovely alternative to a money bag to hold wedding cards.*

## MATERIALS

* 2¾ yds (2.5m) of 1½-inch-wide (4cm) sheer-stripe ribbon in ivory

* 2¾ yds (2.5m) of 1½-inch-wide (4cm) gold-edge sheer ribbon in ivory

* 4 yds (4m) of 2⅝-inch-wide (6.5cm) wire-edge printed sheer ribbon in ivory

* 3 large clusters of hydrangeas with leaves in ivory

* 1 ivy spray, painted gold

* 6 pearl sprays

* 1 gold birdcage, 13 by 10 inches (33 by 25cm), with top opening

* Craft wire

## DIRECTIONS

1. Cut a 1-yard (1m) length of the 1½-inch (4cm) sheer-stripe ribbon. Following the instructions on page 123, make a four-loop bow from this length. Cut a 1-yard (1m) length of the 1½-inch (4cm) sheer ivory ribbon and make a four-loop bow from this length. Wire to the top of the sheer-stripe bow. Cut a 1½-yard (1.5m) length of the 2⅝-inch (6.5cm) printed sheer ivory ribbon and make a six-loop bow from this length. Wire to the other bow. Cut a 15-inch (38cm) length from each of these three ribbons to create a tail and wire it to the bow. Open the top of the birdcage and wire the bow to the left side of the cage top.

2. Wire one hydrangea with long stem and leaves to the center of the bow. Wire the lower portion of the stem to the bottom of the birdcage to ensure that the top stays open. Twist the bow tails and wire to them to the birdcage to hide the flower stem.

3. Cut the gold ivy into four lengths. Wire one length to top flower. Add two pearl sprays.

4. Cut a ½-yard (50cm) length from each of the three ribbons. Make two loops from this length and wire the ribbons together. Wire a 15-inch (38cm) tail of each ribbon to the top of the birdcage. Wire one hydrangea to the center of the bow, then add three pearl sprays and two gold ivy pieces. Twist the tails and wire to the bottom right of the birdcage.

5. Make two loops from half of the remaining 2⅝-inch (6.5cm) printed sheer ivory ribbon and wire to bottom. Add 12-inch (30.5cm) tails of each of the three ribbons. Wire on the last hydrangea, green leaf, gold ivy spray, and pearl spray.

# RIBBON-TRIMMED CAKE SERVING SET AND CHAMPAGNE GLASSES

*Use the same decorative motif—a folded fan made from lace ribbons and bows made from wire-edge ribbons—on the knife, server, and champagne glasses.*

## MATERIALS

* 1½ yds (1.5m) of 2⅛-inch-wide (5.5cm) lace ribbon in white

* 3 yds (3m) of ⅝-inch-wide (1.5cm) wire-edge ribbon in white

* 1½ yds (1.5m) of ⅝-inch-wide (1.5cm) gold-edge sheer ribbon

* 1 yd (1m) of ⅞-inch-wide (2cm) wire-edge sheer novelty ribbon in white and gold

* 8 small gold leaves

* 4 premade mini-swirl ribbon roses in white

* 2 champagne glasses

* Knife and cake server

* Fine craft wire

## DIRECTIONS

1. Cut the 2⅛-inch (5.5cm) white lace ribbon into four 13½-inch (34.5cm) lengths. On one of these lengths, fold ½-inch (1.5cm) pleats from one end to the other. Pinch the bottom edges together and wire in a fan shape. Set aside.

2. Cut the ⅝-inch (1.5cm) white ribbon into four 27-inch (69cm) lengths. Following the instructions on page 123, make a six-loop bow with 3-inch (7.5cm) tails from one of these lengths. Cut the ⅝-inch (1.5cm) gold-edge sheer ribbon into four 13½-inch (34.5cm) lengths. Make a two-loop bow with 2-inch (5cm) tails from one of these lengths. Wire all bows together.

3. Cut the ⅞-inch (2cm) white-and-gold sheer ribbon into four 9-inch (23cm) lengths. Fold one of these lengths in half and wire it to center of bows. Cut off the wire stems from two gold leaves and glue each fanning out from the center. Glue a mini-swirl rose in the center.

4. Glue or wire the bow to the base of the fan from step 1. Trim the ends.

5. Repeat steps 1 to 4 three more times to create four sets of decorations. Wire one each to the cake knife, the server, and the stems of the champagne glasses, using photo as a guide.

# WREATH CENTERPIECE AND GOLD PINWHEEL ORNAMENT FAVORS

*Transform an evergreen wreath into a festive holiday wedding centerpiece with poinsettias, cinnamon sticks, and holiday ribbons in rich velvet and gold mesh.*

More and more brides are choosing to have their weddings during the holiday season. No matter what part of the country you live in, it is a beautiful time of the year to share with those we love. In our mobile society, family and friends are often "home for the holidays" and will then be able to attend the wedding of a loved one. Wedding facilities are beautifully decorated for the holidays and this may help in stretching your floral decorating budget. Rich, luxurious fabrics such as velvets for attendants' attire and tapestries for table settings are especially appealing at this time of the year. So that they will remember your day for years to come, give your guests mementoes of ribbon Christmas ornaments.

# WREATH CENTERPIECE

## MATERIALS

* 5¾ yds (5.5m) of 2⅝-inch-wide (6.5cm) velvet merrow-edge wire ribbon in burgundy

* 6 yds (5.5m) of 2⅝-inch-wide (6.5cm) woven mesh ribbon in gold

* 2 gold fruit, cone, and leaf silk swags about 12 to 14 inches (30.5–35.5cm) long

* 4 gold poinsettia flowers about 8 inches (20.5cm) in diameter

* 18 to 20 long cinnamon sticks

* 18-inch (50cm) artificial green wreath

* Strips of felt, optional

* Glue gun and glue sticks

* Craft wire

## DIRECTIONS

1. Adjust wreath into oval shape. Open up and shape the two swags, nestling each along the long side of the oval wreath. Wire securely to the wreath.

2. Cut two 2-yard (2m) lengths of burgundy velvet ribbon. Following the instructions on page 123, make two six-loop bows with 12-inch (30.5cm) tails from these lengths. Cut two 1½-yard (1.5m) lengths of gold mesh ribbon and make two two-loop bows with 16-inch (40.5cm) tails from these lengths. Wire to the center of the velvet bows, positioning two gold loops at the top. Glue a gold poinsettia in the center of each. Wire each bow at the long end of the centerpiece, allowing the tails to cascade away from the arrangement. Stretch and shape the gold mesh ribbon as desired.

3. Cut two 30-inch (76cm) lengths of both the velvet and the mesh ribbons. Arrange on each long side of the wreath, tucking behind fruits and cones for a natural effect. Wire in place. Tuck the tails behind the bows.

4. Cut two 20-inch (51cm) lengths of gold mesh ribbon and form two two-loop bows from these lengths. Wire to gold poinsettias. Then wire to the center of the long sides of the wreath. Stretch and shape the gold mesh ribbon as desired.

5. Break the cinnamon sticks into 8-inch (20.5cm) lengths and glue broken end into the centerpiece, placing them randomly. Trim ends of ribbon tails.

# Gold Ribbon Bag

## MATERIALS

✤ 2½ yds (2.5m) of 1½-inch-wide (4cm) wire-edge sheer metallic ribbon in gold

✤ ½ yd (50cm) of ⅜-inch-wide (1cm) metallic novelty ribbon in gold

✤ Handful of candy

✤ Glue gun and glue sticks

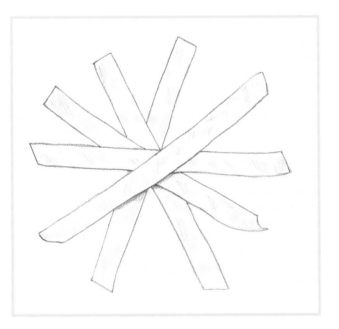

## DIRECTIONS

1. Cut the 1½-inch (4cm) sheer gold metallic ribbon into five 18-inch (50cm) lengths. Criss-cross these lengths over each other to form a star pattern.

2. Place a handful of candy in the center.

3. Gather the ends of the ribbon in the center, forming a small bag. Tie at the center with the ⅜-inch (1cm) metallic novelty ribbon. If necessary, glue the sides of the ribbons together to keep candies from falling out.

4. Cut ends in a point. Fold back edges as desired.

# Gold Pinwheel Ornament Favors

## MATERIALS

❖ 3 yds (3m) of 1½-inch-wide (4cm) wire-edge sheer metallic ribbon in gold

❖ 1 yd (1m) of ⅞-inch-wide (2cm) gold-edge sheer ribbon in gold

❖ ⅜ yd (34.5cm) of ⅛-inch-wide (3mm) metallic novelty ribbon

❖ Novelty ceramic figure painted gold

❖ Needle and thread

❖ Glue gun and glue sticks

## DIRECTIONS

1. Following the instructions for pinwheel folding on page 135, make 26 points from the 1½-inch (4cm) sheer gold metallic ribbon. Tack to form a circle. Fold every other point back slightly.

2. Cut the ⅞-inch (2cm) sheer gold ribbon in half. Mark center and fold each end diagonally to create points. Stitch together and attach to the center of the circle.

3. Glue the ceramic figure to the center, covering the stitching lines.

4. Fold the ⅛-inch (3mm) metallic ribbon in half to form a loop. Attach at the upper edge of the ornament.

*For a Christmas wedding, a ribbon ornament makes a perfect favor. This one features a folding technique that forms a pinwheel design, or further folding transforms it into a hanging ribbon top.*

# Spinning Top Ornament

## MATERIALS

❋ 3 yds (3m) of 1½-inch-wide (4cm) gold-edge taffeta ribbon in burgundy

❋ ¼ yd (23cm) of 1½-inch-wide (4cm) wire-edge sheer metallic ribbon in gold

❋ ¼ yd (23cm) of ⅜-inch-wide (1cm) wire-edge sheer metallic ribbon in gold

❋ 2 yds (2m) of ⅞-inch-wide (2cm) sheer ribbon in gold

❋ Gold bell

❋ Needle and thread

## DIRECTIONS

1. Following the instructions for pinwheel folding on page 135, make 26 points from the 1½-inch (4cm) burgundy taffeta ribbon. Tack to make a circle.

2. To create the spinning top, stitch again, this time on back (flat side) around the center of all the outside points. Pull to tighten, creating a cup. Next, stitch through all the upper points. Pull gently to tighten. Try to make this circle the same diameter as the original center.

3. Fold the 1½-inch (4cm) gold metallic ribbon in half. Baste along the fold, creating a gathering stitch. Gather. Stitch to the lower edge of the top. Stitch the gold bell to the center of the ruffle.

4. Fold the ⅜-inch (1cm) metallic ribbon in half, forming a loop. Stitch to the upper edge of the top.

5. Cut the ⅞-inch (2cm) sheer gold ribbon in half. Following the instructions on page 123, make two six-loop bows from these lengths and stitch to the loop.

# PAPER FAVORS

*When pressed for time, it is still possible to make handmade favors with purchased favor shapes,*
*easily trimmed with enchanting ribbons and premade ribbon roses.*

## MATERIALS FOR ONE FAVOR

* 1½ yds (1.5m) of ⅜-inch-wide (1cm) wire-edge gold metallic ribbon

* 1½ yds (1.5m) of ⅝-inch-wide (1.5cm) sheer ribbon

* 4 (1 pkg) premade small gold roses

* Assorted purchased paper favors

## DIRECTIONS

1. Embellish the paper favors with ribbons and roses, using photo as a guide.

2. To curl the ⅜-inch (1cm) gold metallic ribbon, wrap it tightly around a pencil. Remove carefully.

*What do I get*

*from loving you?*
*Loving. You.*

—John Roger

# PEARL FRAMES

*Pearls by the yard and ribbon bows turn a plain purchased frame into a wedding-day treasure.*

## Ivory Frame

### MATERIALS

- ½ yd (50cm) of 1½-inch-wide (4cm) sheer gold-merrow-edge wire ribbon in ivory

- 6½ yds (6m) of thin pearl string in ivory

- 7½-by-5½-inch (19-by-14cm) rectangular frame

- White spray paint, optional

- Glue gun and glue sticks

### DIRECTIONS

1. Remove the glass and the cardboard easel backing from the frame. If desired, spray-paint the frame white; let dry completely.

2. Beginning on the inside of the frame, cut a length of pearl string to fit. Glue in place. Turn frame one-quarter turn and cut another length of pearls. Glue in place. Repeat for remaining two sides. Working one row at a time, repeat this process until the entire top and sides of the frame are completely covered. Spot-glue any stray pearl strings or fill gaps as needed.

3. Following the instructions on page 123, make a two-loop bow with a center loop from the 1½-inch (4cm) sheer ivory ribbon. Glue the bow to the top of the frame, arranging tails as shown.

4. Replace the glass and the cardboard backing.

*The best way to hold a man is in your arms.*

— Mae West

# $\mathscr{P}$EACH $\mathscr{F}$RAME

## MATERIALS

❖ 16 inches (30.5cm) of ⅛-inch-wide (3mm) satin ribbon in peach

❖ 1 yd (1m) of 1½-inch-wide (4cm) wire-edge sheer ribbon in peach

❖ 1 premade ribbon lily in peach

❖ 6½ yds (6m) of thin pearl string in peach

❖ 6½-by-6½-inch (16.5-by-16.5cm) square frame

❖ White spray paint, optional

❖ Glue gun and glue sticks

## DIRECTIONS

1. Remove the glass and the cardboard easel backing from the frame. If desired, spray-paint the frame white; let dry completely.

2. Beginning on the inside of the frame, cut a length of pearl string to fit. Glue in place. Turn frame one-quarter turn and cut another length of pearls. Glue in place. Repeat for remaining two sides. Working one row at a time, repeat this process until the entire top and sides of the frame are completely covered. Spot-glue any stray pearl strings or fill gaps as needed.

3. Cut 4-inch (10cm) lengths of the ⅛-inch (3mm) peach satin ribbon and glue diagonally across each corner of the pearl-covered frame, beginning at the inside and wrapping the excess to the back. Following the instructions on page 123, make a four-loop bow with 8-inch (20.5cm) tails from the 1½-inch (4cm) sheer peach ribbon. Glue the premade lily to the center of the bow. Glue the bow to the top left of the frame, arranging tails as shown.

4. Replace the glass and the cardboard backing.

# Selecting a Month to Marry

Marry when the year is new,
Always loving, kind, and true.

When February birds do mate
You may wed, nor dread your fate.

If you wed when March winds blow,
Joy and sorrow both you'll know.

Marry in April when you can,
Joy for maiden and for man.

Marry in the month of May,
You will surely rue the day.

Marry when June roses blow,
Over land and sea you'll go.

They who in July do wed
Must labor always for their bread.

Whoever wed in August be,
Many a change are sure to see.

Marry in September's shine,
Your living will be rich and fine.

If in October you do marry,
Love will come, but riches tarry.

If you wed in bleak November
Only joy will come, remember.

When December's snow falls fast,
Marry, and true love will last.

# DOILY CONES

*Rolled cones of doilies trimmed with ribbon roses hold flower petals to toss at the departing bride and groom.*

## MATERIALS FOR ONE CONE

* ½ yd (50cm) of 2⅝-inch-wide (6.5cm) floral satin ribbon in yellow or pink

* 1 yd (1m) of ⅛-inch-wide (3mm) satin ribbon in pink or yellow

* 8 inches (20.5cm) of ⅜-inch-wide (1cm) satin ribbon in pink or yellow

* 1 pkg of ribbon rose garland in white

* 10 (1 pkg) premade small ribbon roses in white

* 8-inch (20.5cm) pearl string in white, cut in half

* Two 5-to-6-inch (13–15cm) paper doilies

* Craft wire

## DIRECTIONS

1. Cut three lengths of the 2⅝-inch (6.5cm) floral satin ribbon and glue to a doily, overlapping the edge of each length by ⅛ inch (3mm). Turn over and glue the second doily in place, aligning it so it matches the pattern of the other doily. Trim the edge to within ⅛ inch (3mm) with pinking shears.

2. Cut a 16-inch (40.5cm) length of the ⅛-inch (3mm) satin ribbon. Make a tassel from this length by forming it into a four-loop bow with 2-inch (5cm) tails. Wire the bow center, adding in the two 4-inch (10cm) lengths of pearl string at the center. Fasten and fold in half and wire again; cut off wire ends.

3. Fold the doily into a cone shape, creasing under one end to create straight front edge. Glue the tassel in place and glue the seam closed.

4. Glue the rose garland in place along the seam, beginning with a rose at the top of the tassel and bringing excess ribbon into cone.

5. Glue the ⅜-inch (1cm) satin ribbon at the top of the cone to form a handle; glue ends to inside. Cut the remaining ⅛-inch (3mm) satin ribbon in half and make two bows from these lengths. Glue to the outside of each handle. Glue one small rose on the inside of the handle and two each on the outside. Glue the remaining four roses around the top of the tassel to finish.

# CANDY OR POTPOURRI BAGS

*Say "thank you" to your guests for sharing your special day*
*with ribbon bags filled with candies or fragrant potpourri.*

## Sachet Bag

### MATERIALS FOR ONE BAG

❀ 2 yds (2m) of ⅜-inch-wide (1cm) wire-edge sheer metallic ribbon in gold

❀ ½ yd (50cm) of 4-inch-wide (10cm) wire-edge sheer ribbon in ivory

❀ ¾ yd (69cm) of ⅝-inch-wide (1.5cm) single-face satin ribbon in azalea

❀ 1 yd (1m) of ⅝-inch-wide (1.5cm) novelty trim in ivory

❀ ¼ yd (23cm) of ⅞-inch-wide (2cm) single-face satin ribbon in azalea

❀ Candy or potpourri

### DIRECTIONS

1. Cut the ⅜-inch (1cm) sheer metallic gold ribbon into four 18-inch (50cm) lengths. Place one length along each finished edge of the 4-inch (10cm) sheer ivory ribbon and stitch in place. Stitch the third length of ribbon in the center of the 4-inch (10cm) ribbon, parallel to the other rows of ribbon.

2. Measure down 9 inches (23cm) from the cut edge of the 4-inch (10cm) sheer ribbon and mark. Measure and mark 2 inches (5cm), 4 inches (10cm), and 6 inches (15cm) away from the marking on both sides for placement lines (see illustration on page 118).

3. Cut the ⅝-inch (1.5cm) azalea satin ribbon into six 4½-inch (11.5cm) lengths and stitch these lengths on all six placement lines.

4. Cut the ⅝-inch (1.5cm) ivory novelty trim into six 4½-inch (11.5cm) lengths and one 9-inch (23cm) length. Place along the lower edges of the ⅝-inch (1.5cm) azalea satin ribbon and stitch in place.

5. Fold the 4-inch (10cm) sheer ivory ribbon from step 1 in half with wrong sides together and stitch along one edge. Encase the top edges with the ⅞-inch (2cm) azalea satin ribbon and stitch in place. Attach the trim to the upper edge. Stitch the remaining edge of the 4-inch (10cm) sheer ivory ribbon, forming a bag.

6. Fill the bag with candy or potpourri and tie the upper edge in a bow with the remaining length of the ⅜-inch (1cm) sheer metallic gold ribbon.

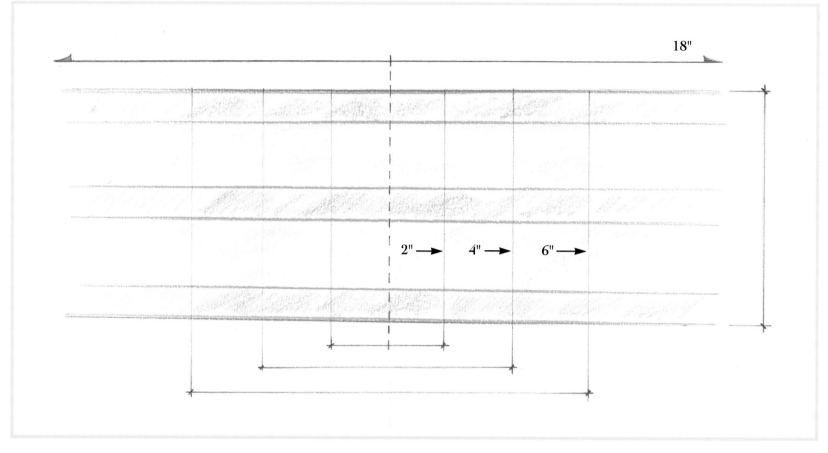

18"

2" → 4" → 6" →

Directions for Sachet Bag

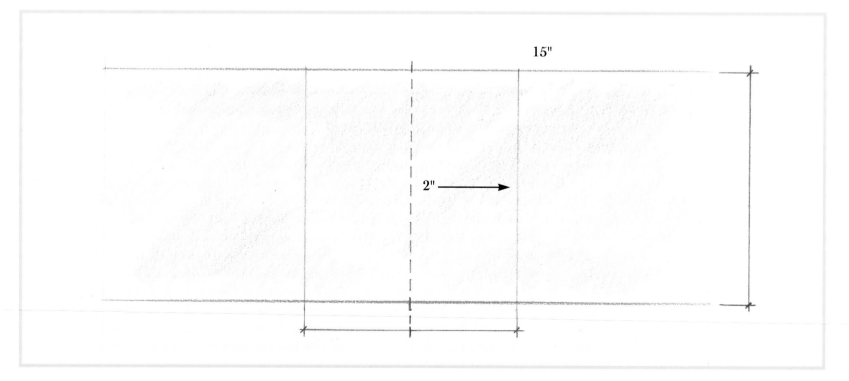

15"

2" →

Directions for "Firecracker" Bag

# "Firecracker" Bag

## MATERIALS FOR ONE BAG

❈ 30 inches (76cm) of 4-inch-wide (10cm) wire-edge sheer ribbon in ivory

❈ ½ yd (50cm) of ⅜-inch-wide (1cm) wire-edge sheer metallic ribbon in gold, cut in half

❈ ½ yd (50cm) of ⅞-inch-wide (2cm) single-face satin ribbon in azalea

❈ ½ yd (50cm) of ⅝-inch-wide (1.5cm) novelty trim in ivory, cut in half

❈ 3 yds (3m) of ⅛-inch-wide (3mm) single-face satin ribbon in azalea

❈ Candy or potpourri

## DIRECTIONS

1. Cut the 4-inch (10cm) sheer ivory ribbon in half. Mark the center of each length. Measure and mark 2 inches (5cm) away from either side of center marking. Cut the ⅜-inch (1cm) sheer gold metallic ribbon in half and stitch each length along the new markings on the sheer ivory ribbon (see illustration on page 118).

2. With wrong sides together, stitch the two lengths of the 4-inch (10cm) sheer ivory ribbon along one finished edge.

3. Baste along the center of the ⅞-inch (2cm) azalea satin ribbon, forming a gathering stitch. Gather the ribbon and pin along the center marking. Stitch in place.

4. Finish the raw edges at top and bottom by forming a narrow hem and stitching novelty trim on top of hem. Stitch the other side closed.

5. Fill the bag with candy or potpourri. Cut the ⅛-inch (3mm) azalea satin ribbon into six 18-inch (50cm) lengths and use three lengths to tie each end of the bag closed.

# CHAPTER FIVE

# Tying *the* Knot

*I would like to have engraved inside*

*every wedding band "Be kind to one*

*another." This is the Golden Rule of*

*marriage and the secret of making*

*love last through the years.*

—Randolph Ray

To those of you who have read *Offray: The Splendor of Ribbon,* this chapter will seem familiar. I am repeating some of the techniques from that book and including some new ones so you can expand your knowledge of ribbon usage. When you look over the instructions for specific projects in other chapters, you will see materials lists for each of them as well as references to the general techniques found in this section. Before you begin, be sure to have your basic supplies on hand. These include the following:

* Scissors
* Needle and thread
* Glue gun and glue sticks
* Green floral tape
* Needle-nose pliers
* Ruler
* Tape measure
* Pinking sheers
* Masking tape
* Covered floral wire

Your choice of ribbon type will make a big difference to the finished look. If you have done much ribbon crafting, you know that there are two basic types of ribbon from which to choose. If you substitute ribbons for those called for in these projects, be sure to select the correct type of ribbon. A good rule to follow is that woven ribbons (which have finished selvages or edges) are for stitch-down applications and may be washed or dry-cleaned. Craft or floral ribbons (which are cut from wide fabrics into ribbon widths) are glued or wired to a particular project and are not to be washed or dry-cleaned.

There are also many types of wire-edge ribbons available, and they, too, fall into two categories. In woven wire-edge ribbons, the wire is woven in as part of the construction of the ribbon. In merrow-edge wire ribbons, the wire is stitched to the ribbon by a merrowing (serging) process. This merrowing process gives the ribbon a distinctive, "heavier" edge, which makes this type of ribbon suitable for floral arrangements such as centerpieces, decorative wreaths, and pew bows. A woven wire-edge ribbon makes a lovely loopy bow or it can be turned into beautiful flowers for corsages, headpieces, and other decorative items as seen throughout this book.

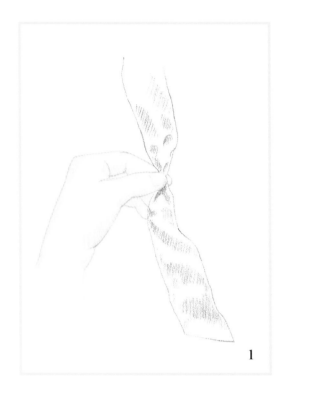

**1**

To fasten a bow with wire, fold an 18-inch (50cm) length of wire in half. Place the folded wire underneath the chosen ribbon and wrap the wire around the center, inserting the wire ends through the loop to tighten. Pull the wire ends to secure, bringing one end around center again at back. To tighten, twist the bow—*not* the wire—a few times.

## TWO-LOOP BOW AND VARIATIONS

Cut a length of ribbon as specified in the project instructions. Wrap the ribbon back and forth, forming two loops with tails. Glue a small strip of ribbon around the ribbon loops to hold it in place. Ease the ribbon tail to the back of the bow.

For four-, six-, eight-, ten-, and twelve-loop bows, simply increase the number of loops before securing the center strip.

**Note:** When using ombré ribbon, results will differ depending on which side of the ribbon you work. Experiment with this for interesting color variations.

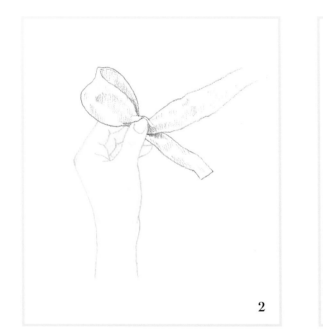

**2**

**3**

**4**

## FLORIST BOW

Begin by leaving a tail of at least 8 inches (20.5cm), and pinch at the center between thumb and index finger. Bring the ribbon up and back down, forming a loop. Gather firmly between thumb and index finger. Twist the ribbon, then bring it down and back up to form another loop, and again pinch and twist it into place between thumb and index finger. Repeat the process of forming loops until you have made the desired number of loops. Secure the loops by wrapping the center with wire. Fasten wire and twist the bow a few turns in the same direction to finish. Adjust bow loops. Notch or trim the ends. Add a center loop, if desired.

## LOOP AND TAIL SHAPES

Form loop and tail shapes by making one or two loops folded back on themselves, with one streamer (usually about double the length of loops) extending from the same end. Finish by wiring at center folds.

## TRIMMING RIBBON ENDS

To prevent fraying and ensure a proper finished appearance, always trim the straight cut end of the ribbon. There are three styles of cuts to choose from:

❋ Upside down V: Lightly fold the ribbon in half and cut cleanly from the outer edge toward the fold. This method results in a symmetrical look.

❋ Point: Lightly fold the ribbon in half and cut cleanly from inner fold out to edges. This cut can be rounded or trimmed if desired.

❋ Angled cut: Make one clean cut from one ribbon edge up or down to the other edge in a 45-degree angle.

## Attaching a Flower to a Stem

Cut stem wire to desired length. With needle-nose pliers, bend a small loop at one end of the wire. (This loop will be concealed with the stamens or in the center of the flower and will help prevent flower head from being easily removed.) Attach stem wire to stamens with floral tape. If not using stamens, conceal the loop in the center of a petal. Wrap petal to stem wire below the loop. Attach with fine floral wire, then cover with green floral tape.

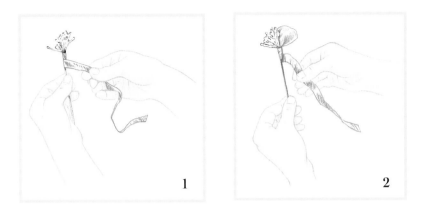

## Folded Leaf

Cut ribbon to desired length. Mark center of ribbon and fold each end diagonally to center mark. At lower edge, fold each side of ribbon toward center. Gently pleat fullness at lower edge to center. Twist tightly to hold. Secure twist with floral tape. To attach leaf, use floral tape and wrap on twisted end of ribbon.

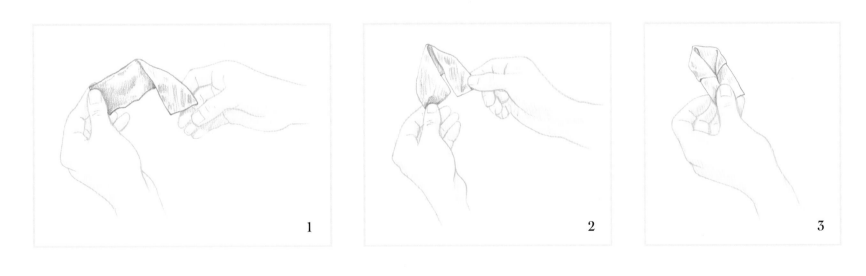

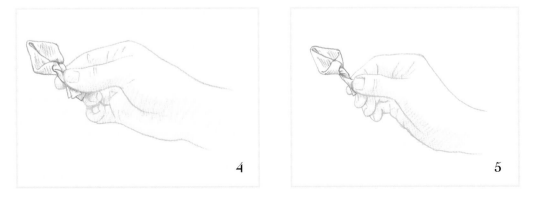

## PULLED LEAF OR PETAL

For each leaf or petal, cut wire-edge ribbon to desired length. Fold in half. Gather one edge of ribbon by pulling both ends of the wire from the cut ends at the same time; this prevents you from accidentally pulling the wire out of the ribbon. Push all gathers to the center of the ribbon. Overlap the ends of the ribbon and, with wire exposed, tightly wrap the ends together to hold. If desired, apply a small line of glue down the center seam to hold the leaf or petal closed. The ends of the leaf or petal can be left rounded or pinched to a point as desired.

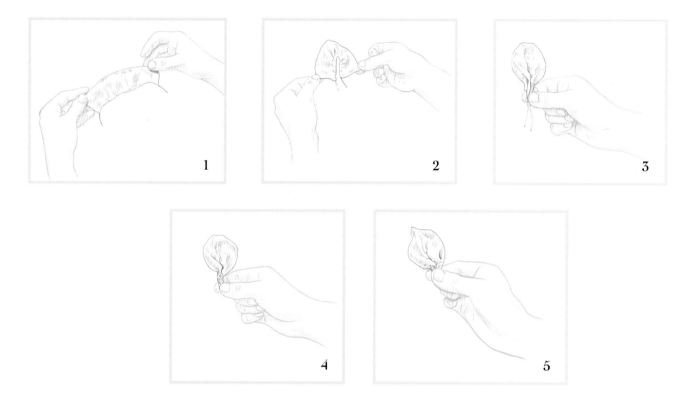

## ROLLED PETAL

Cut ribbon to desired length. Fold in half. With a knitting needle or the equivalent, gently roll each edge at the fold. Roll at a 45-degree angle. When attaching the petal, gently pleat the lower edge so petal will "cup." Place petals with rolled edges facing away from the center of the flower.

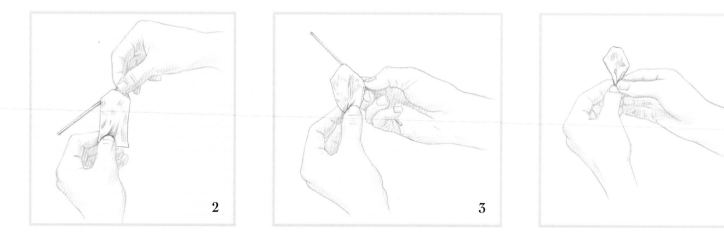

## Rolled Petal Rose

Cut five 5-inch (13cm) lengths of ribbon. Fold each length in half. Roll folded edge over knitting needle on each side to curl the petals. To assemble, cut a 3-inch (7.5cm) length of 16- to 18-gauge floral wire. Wire a pearl cluster stamen to one end of the floral wire using fine wire. Finger-pleat the lower edge of the first petal and attach the wire onto the stem wire. Repeat this process for the other four petals. Cover the wire with green floral tape. For rosebuds, eliminate the pearl cluster stamens and wire three petals each onto a 3-inch (7.5cm) length of 16- or 18-gauge covered wire.

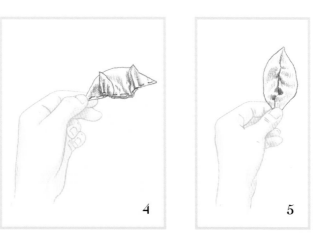

1

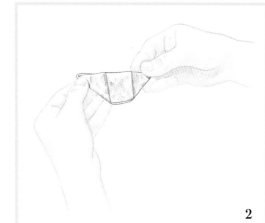

2

## Stitched "Boat" Leaf or Petal

Cut ribbon to desired length. Fold in half. Fold corners up at 45-degree angle (resulting in a boatlike shape). With needle and thread (knotted at one end), begin stitching at top edge of fold through all thicknesses down angled edge, across lower edge, and up the other side. Gently pull stitches to gather ribbon into a some- what straight line. Knot to secure. Trim excess ribbon from folds. Open ribbon to make leaf or petal.

**Note:** Experiment with ombré ribbon for interesting color variations.

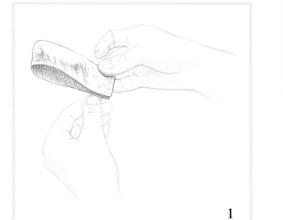

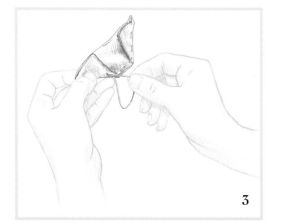

3

4

5

## STITCHED AND GATHERED PETALS

Cut ribbon to desired length. Measure and mark on the ribbon the correct length of each petal. With needle and matching thread, stitch ribbon as illustrated. Every two to three sections, gently but firmly gather the stitches together to make petals. Repeat along entire length of ribbon. Pull all gathers together firmly. Knot thread to secure. Arrange petals into a circle and join. If desired, sew across space at center to close. Thread stamen wire through center of flower and secure in place. If necessary, use floral tape to attach flower to stem wire.

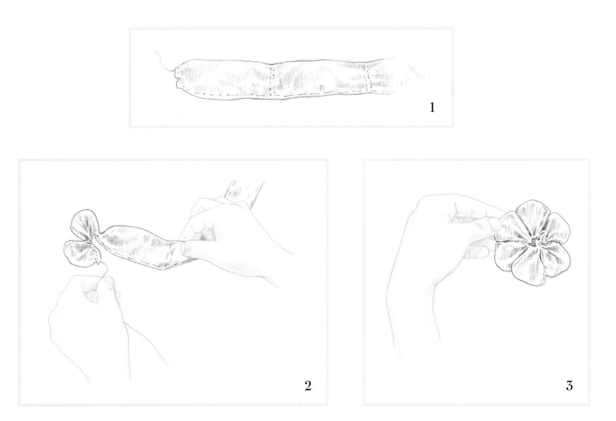

## CAMELLIA

Cut a 50-inch (127cm) length of ⅞-inch (2cm) wide wire-edge ribbon. Measure and mark as follows: three 3-inch (7.5cm) petals, four 4-inch (10cm) petals, and five 5-inch (13cm) petals. With sewing needle and doubled thread, stitch down one side of petal, across bottom, and up the other side of petal. Repeat across entire length of ribbon for each petal marking. Stop peri-odically and tightly gather stitches into petals. (See steps 1 and 2, above.) When stitching is complete, gather all petals firmly and knot to tie off. To assemble flower, start with the 3-inch (7.5cm) petals: wrap into a circle, then stitch to hold. Wrap the 4-inch (10cm) petals around the 3-inch (7.5cm) petal cluster. Sew in place. Repeat for the 5-inch (13cm) petals. Insert a pearl stamen cluster in the center.

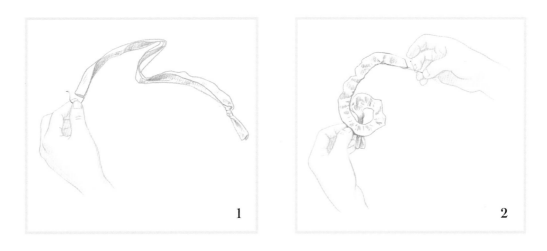

## FANCY ROSE

Cut ribbon to desired length. Knot one end, and pull knot firmly toward end to secure. Hold ribbon at opposite end and poke out wires from both sides of ribbon. Fold ribbon in half lengthwise and push ribbon down length of wire toward the knot, forming a tightly gathered ruffle. Keep both layers together as one. Form rose by rolling gathered edge around knot. Continue wrapping ribbon around to achieve desired look (see above). Secure the ends.

## PULLED OR GATHERED ROSE

Cut ribbon to desired length. Knot one end, and pull knot firmly toward end to secure. From opposite side, gently pull one wire, slowly gathering ribbon along that edge. Continue gathering until entire side is completely ruffled and curling naturally. Wrap gathered ribbon around knotted end, forming a bud. Continue wrapping lightly so ribbon flares out and acquires an open rose effect. Tie wires together and trim. Adjust shape by fluffing or crumpling.

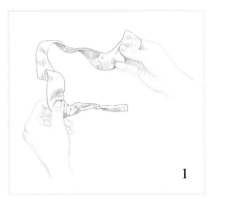

1

2

3

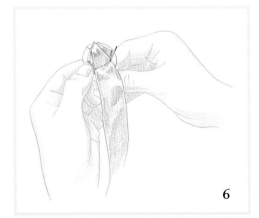

1

2

## CABBAGE ROSE

Cut a circle of buckram 1 to 2 inches (2.5–5cm) in diameter. Slash buckram circle to center, overlap slashed edges to form a cone shape, and stitch overlapped edges in place. Cut ribbon to desired length and turn under one end. Place ribbon across cone center and stitch in place along three sides of ribbon. Fold ribbon diagonally across cone to top right corner. Stitch in place. Continue folding diagonally and stitching in place, being careful not to completely cover center or previous folds. When buckram is completely covered, stitch ribbon ends to back of circle.

3

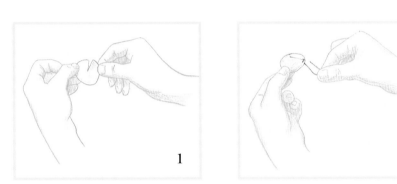

4

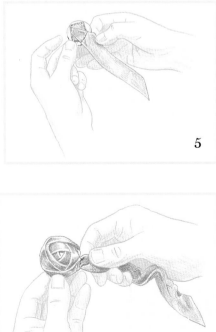

5

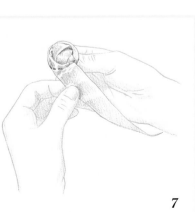

6

7

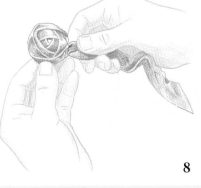

8

# FOLDED ROSE

Cut ribbon to desired length. To form rose center, fold down one end of ribbon on a diagonal and roll folded end about six turns. Stitch at base to secure. Begin forming petals by folding top edge away from you at a 45-degree angle, parallel to center. Using tacked base as a pivot, roll across fold, loosely at top and tightly at base, forming a cone shape. Tack at base to secure. Continue to fold, roll, and tack, shaping the rose as you work. Wind tightly to form a bud shape; winding loosely creates a more full-blown rose. Finish by turning under raw end and tacking to base. (If using craft ribbon, do not sew rose. Using glue gun, apply tiny dots of glue as you fold and roll to secure rose.) Secure with floral wire wrapped tightly around base.

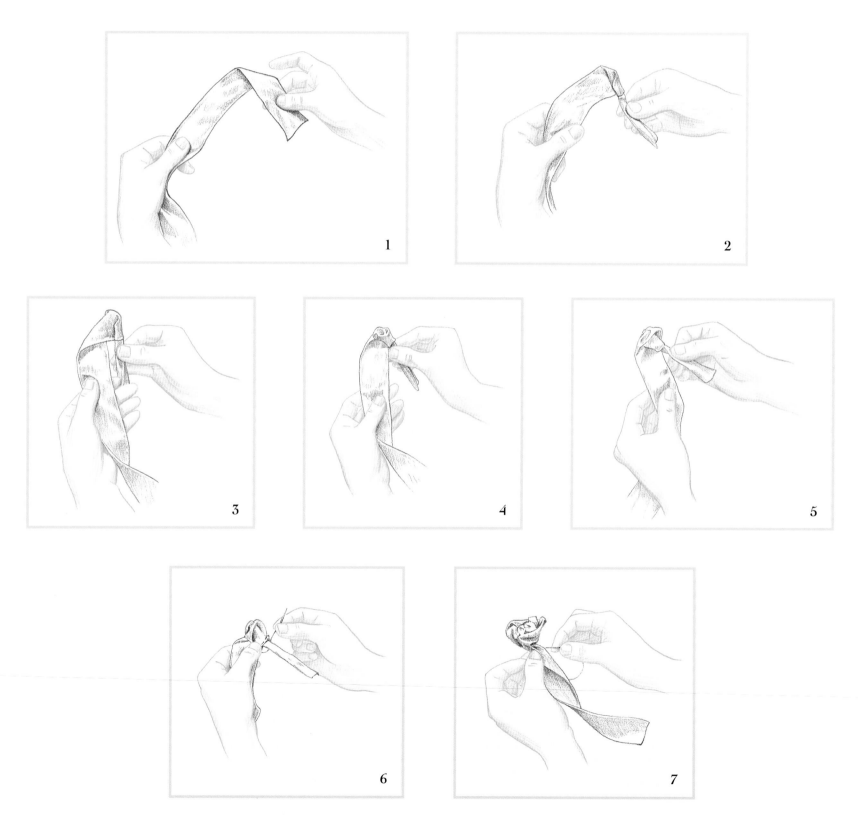

# Trillium

Cut a 3-inch (7.5cm) length of covered floral wire for the stem. Using paddle wire or floral tape, attach a pearl cluster stamen to stem wire. Cut three 5-inch (13cm) lengths of ribbon. Fold one in half lengthwise to mark center, then fold edges of ribbon on the diagonal to both sides of center. Slide center edges of ribbon to curve the petal tip. Tack folded-down ribbon edges to lower edge of ribbon to secure curved tip. With knitting needle, roll each edge of petal to center of petal. Repeat for remaining two ribbon lengths. To assemble flower, arrange the three petals around the pearl cluster stamen. Secure petals to stem using paddle wire and cover raw edges with floral tape.

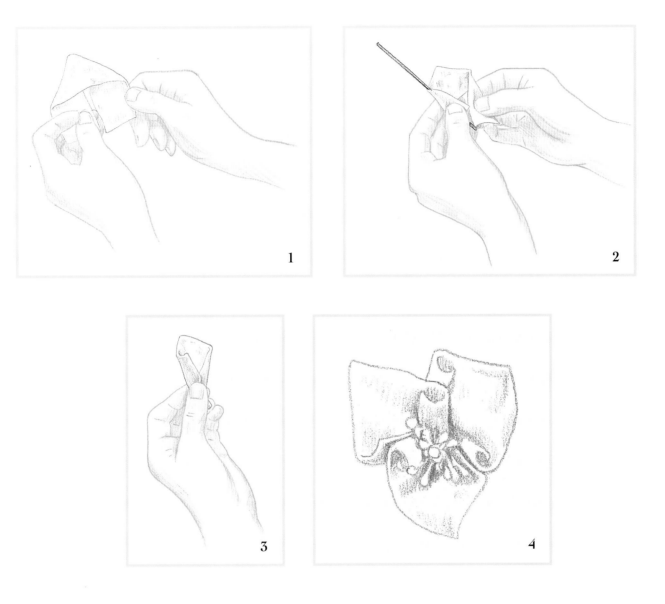

## ORCHID

Cut a 3-inch (7.5cm) length of covered floral wire for stem. Using paddle wire or floral tape, attach a pearl cluster stamen to stem wire. Cut two 7-inch (18cm) lengths and three 6-inch (15cm) lengths of ribbon per flower. For one petal, fold ribbon in half and push wire from each end of one side of ribbon. Gather ribbon evenly and tightly along wire. Overlap raw edges and wrap ends with wire to form the petal. If desired, secure the center overlap of ribbon with a small amount of glue to close center opening of petal. For the 7-inch (18cm) petals, leave edges rounded. For the 6-inch (15cm) petals, pinch end into a point. To assemble, overlap two 7-inch (18cm) petals and attach with paddle wire to the pearl cluster stamen. Next, attach one 6-inch (15cm) petal opposite the first two petals. Then attach a 6-inch (15cm) petal to either side of the center 6-inch (15cm) petal as shown. Cover all raw edges with green floral tape.

## CALLA LILY

Cut a 6-inch (15cm) length of ribbon, a 2-inch (5cm) length of chenille stem, and a 3-inch (7.5cm) length of floral wire. Fold the ribbon in half lengthwise to mark center, then fold edges of ribbon on the diagonal to both sides of center. Slide center edges of ribbon slightly to curve the petal tip. Tack ribbon in place. (This is the back side of the petal.) Turn to front. Fold front edges together and roll edges over a knitting needle. Insert the cut chenille stem into the center. Gather edges together. Wire to the cut length of floral wire. Cover raw edges with green floral tape.

1

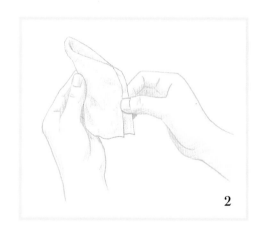

2

3

4

The techniques described below for weaving provide more opportunities to be creative with ribbon. From these techniques you will be able to create your own fabric for various projects, or simply embellish parts of projects. Once you have tried these methods and realize how quick and easy they are, there will be no limit to the uses you will find for them. For variety, change the widths and types of ribbons in each project.

## BASIC WEAVE AND VARIATIONS

Cut lengths of ribbon and fusible interfacing as specified in individual projects. Place fusible interfacing, fusible side up, on a pinnable work surface—a purchased pinning board, an ironing board, or fabric-covered cardboard. Draw the required dimensions on the interfacing. Place the first vertical length of ribbon (the warp) on the interfacing, aligning edge of ribbon with line on interfacing. Butt edges of remaining warp ribbons and pin at upper end of ribbons. Angle pins away from work to keep pins clear of iron when fusing. Weave horizontal lengths of ribbons (the weft) one over, one under the vertical ribbons, continuing across the layout. When row is complete, push weft ribbon up to top seam marking, making sure the ribbon is straight and taut. Pin ends in place. Continue weaving weft ribbons until project is complete. Before starting a new row, be sure the previous row is pulled taut and straight, edges butting with previous weft ribbon. Fuse ribbons to interfacing following manufacturer's instructions. Machine-stitch along outer edges of ribbons on all four sides to secure ribbons in place. Stitching is especially important with metallic ribbons since they do not fuse well.

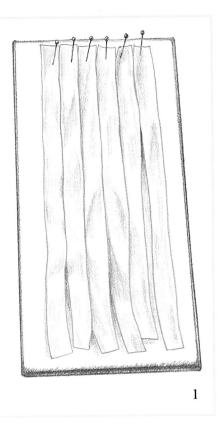

1

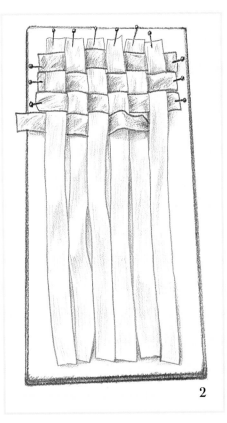

2

# Three-Dimensional Ribbon Weaving

To form a tumbling-blocks pattern that has a three-dimensional look, one ribbon is used for the warp, and two different ribbons are used for each set of the diagonal weaving. Ribbons in three colors or three different designs or textures create a very striking effect. To begin, pin fusible interfacing, fusible side up, to an ironing board or padded work surface.

WARP - These are the lengthwise ribbons that are placed right side up onto fusible interfacing with edges touching.

WEFT 1 - There are two sets of weft ribbons; the first set is woven from the upper left to the lower right in this order:

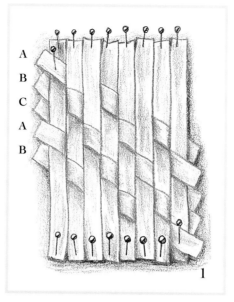

Row A - over 1 warp, under 2 warps, over 1, under 2, over 1, under 2, and so on.

Row B - under 1 warp, over 1 warp, under 2 warps, over 1, under 2, over 1, under 2, and so on

Row C - under 2 warps, over 1 warp, under 2 warps, over 1, under 2, and so on

Repeat rows A, B, C across length of piece. (See diagram 1.)

WEFT 2 - The second set of weft ribbons is woven from the lower left to the upper right. Think only of weaving this ribbon over and under the other weft ribbon. Try to ignore the warp ribbons as you weave the second set of weft ribbons. The warp ribbons will automatically be included in your design as you weave weft 2 over and under weft 1. Weave in this order:

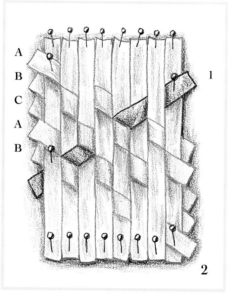

Row 1 - over 1 weft (or ribbon B), under 2 weft ribbons (ribbons A and C), over 1 (ribbon B), under 2 (ribbons A and C), over 1 (ribbon B), and so on

Row 2 - under 2 weft ribbons (B and A), over 1 weft (ribbon C), under 2 weft ribbons (ribbons B and A), over 1 weft (ribbon C), and so on

Row 3 - under 2 weft ribbons (C and B), over 1 weft (ribbon A), under 2 weft ribbons (C and B), over 1 weft ribbon (ribbon A), and so on

Repeat rows 1, 2, and 3 across length of piece.
(See diagrams 2 and 3.)

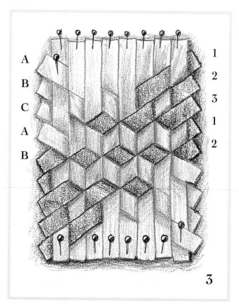

# General Pinwheel Folding Technique

Cut ribbon to desired length. Following the diagram, proceed with steps 1 through 6, starting at right end of ribbon. This will make two folded sections or one point. Repeat from step 3 until you have the necessary number of points (about 26 for the pro-jects in this book). Tack bottom points together as needed to hold in place. On the last point, fold under ¼ inch (6mm) and stitch in place. Tack last bottom point to beginning bottom point to form a circle.

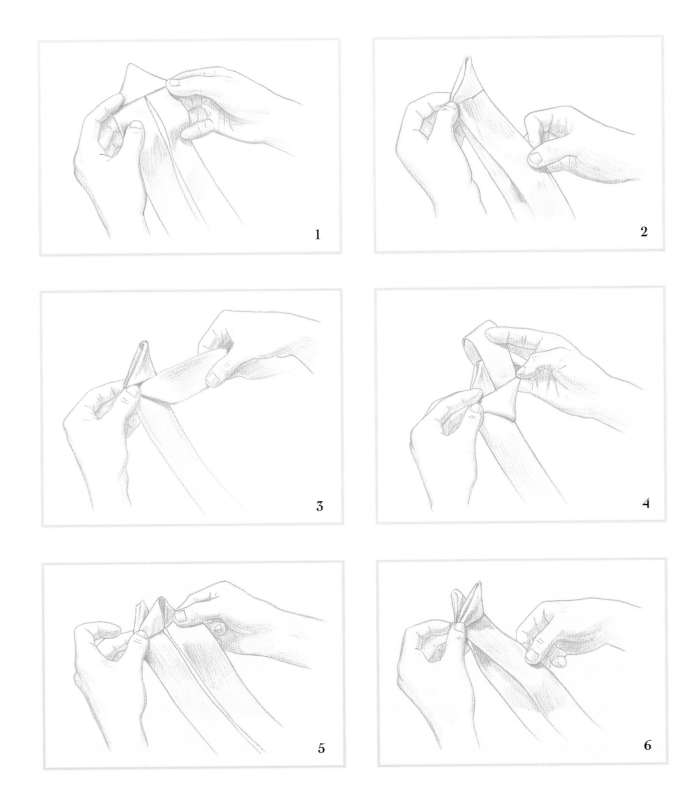

# Bride's Wedding Planner

The time between your engagement and wedding is one of great anticipation and excitement. No matter what size wedding you are having, there are many details to pay attention to. Unless you are planning to hire a wedding consultant, these plans and details are left to you, your fiancé, and your families. There is no hard and fast rule any longer about who pays for what. Today it is not uncommon for the bride and groom to pay for the wedding themselves. Before any planning begins, it is wise to have a budget in mind to guide you as you create your perfect wedding. The following is a general outline you may want to use to plan your wedding. By being organized, you and your fiancé can enjoy this crazy, hectic time together. So set your wedding date... and—on your mark, get set, go!

## With Twelve Months To Go...

❋ Now would be a great time to buy or make a planning book. Why not personalize one with your favorite picture of you and your fiancé on the cover, so when things get frantic you can take a look at the picture and remember why you're going through with this.

❋ Establish your budget! At this point you may not know what everything will cost, but it is a very good idea to know what you can afford.

❋ Visit potential wedding and reception locations. If you are getting married at the height of wedding season, the longer you wait, the fewer locations will be available.

❋ Appoint your bridal attendants, keeping in mind that being an attendant involves costs and responsibilities. You'll want to select family members or close friends you can count on.

❋ Determine the style or theme of your wedding, including colors. Will it be modern or traditional? Will it be formal or informal?

❋ Book the "supporting cast": florist, musicians, and photographer. If you are unfamiliar with these professionals, visit bridal fairs and special events to see portfolios. You may also consult your married friends and family members to see if they have any personal recommendations.

## With Nine Months To Go...

❋ With your fiancé, begin compiling names and addresses of guests.

❋ Order your dress and accessories. If you are planning to personally create or embellish your accessories, start to do it now while you have time to enjoy selecting ribbons and learning new techniques.

❋ You and your fiancé should choose the officiant for your wedding and make an appointment to meet with that person. You should think about your vows and whether you'd like to use the standard vows or write your own.

## With Six Months To Go...

❋ Shop with attendants for their attire.

❋ Register with bridal registries in stores in locations accessible to both families and friends.

❋ Order invitations, announcements, and personal stationery, and book calligrapher.

## With Three Months To Go...

❋ Finalize guest list. If you are expecting out-of-town guests, arrange for local accommodations.

❋ If you have not already done so, book your honeymoon. This is important; after all the excitement of the wedding, the two of you will need this special time together.

## With Two Months To Go...

❋ Address invitations, to be mailed four to six weeks before the wedding.

❋ Finalize all details with "supporting cast."

❋ Have you ordered your wedding cake? Now would be a good time!

* Within the next two weeks, have your final fitting and then stick with a healthy diet and exercise plan!

* Plan your rehearsal dinner and attendants' lunch. (You can indulge a little here!)

* Purchase gifts for your attendants. Be creative, and don't forget to wrap them with beautiful ribbons.

* Make wedding favors—there are so many ideas to choose from in this book.

### With One Month To Go…

* The Big Day is quickly approaching—it's time to get the marriage license and blood test (if required).

* Make wedding-day transportation arrangements.

* Send out thank-you notes for gifts as they are received.

### With One Week To Go…

* Plan seating arrangements; give a head count to the caterer.

* This is the time to go over all final details with the florist, photographer, and musicians.

* Treat yourself and your fiancé to a much-deserved massage!

### The Big Day…

* Your organization has paid off and you are ready. You left enough time to do your hair, make-up, and nails, and even to have a relaxing bath.

* Have fun, and congratulations!

# About the Ribbons Used in This Book

Many retailers that carry Offray and Lion ribbons will special order them for you. To assist you in finding the Offray and Lion ribbons used in this book, I have identified the distinctive ribbons that have been included in many of the projects. In addition, Offray's classic satin ribbons, feather-edge satin ribbons, wire-edge taffeta ribbons, wire-edge ombré ribbons, and premade ribbon roses and other flowers were used. These can be found at most fabric and craft stores.

MW SKYE, a merrowed wired sheer pastel plaid, and MW CARA, a merrowed wired sheer ribbon, were used in the Breakaway Centerpiece and Favors, and in the Wedding Shower Umbrella.

WIRE-EDGE ARABESQUE, a satin-edged sheer ribbon that's available in many lovely colors, was used on the Wire Mesh Purses, the Mothers' Corsages, the Flower Girl Headpiece, and the Pew Bows.

WIRE-EDGE CHARISMA, a pastel wired ribbon, was used for many of the flowers, and for the Wire Mesh Purses.

MW WINDY, a wide, slightly crinkled sheer that is available in white and ecru, was used to make the flowers on the Bride's Shoes and Garter and to decorate the Pew Bows, the Broom, the Bridal Chair Back Swag, and the Wedding Wreath.

MW ANNIE, a merrowed wired sheer floral print, was used for the Wedding Wreath and the Bridal Chair Back Swag.

WIRE-EDGE SALUTATION is a white and gold ribbon with the words "with love" woven into it. This ribbon was used on the Broom and the sublime version of the Pew Bows.

WIRE-EDGE SULTY, a crinkled gold metallic ribbon, was used to decorate the Broom.

MW JILLIAN, a wide sheer floral print in pastel colors, was used to create the Bridesmaid Headpiece.

If you would like a set of swatches of the ribbons used, send $5.00 to:

Offray Bridal Ribbons
Department PM
857 Willow Circle
Hagerstown, MD 21740

*Please allow four to six weeks for delivery.*

# Sources

Bill's Flower Market, Inc.
(Silk and dry flowers)
816 6th Avenue
New York, NY 10010
(212) 889-8154

City Blossoms
(Stand-up bouquet, mesh bags,
and flowers)
17 Battery Place
New York, NY 10004
(212) 269-8190

Enterprise Art
(Beads and jewelry findings)
P.O. Box 2918
Largo, FL 34649
(813) 536-1492

General Bead
637 Minna Street
San Francisco, CA 94103
(415) 255-2323

Lacis
(Orange blossom kits)
3163 Adeline Street
Berkeley, CA 94703
(510) 843-7178

Mine Hill Seed Beads
(Gloves and pebble beads)
P.O. Box 1060
Janesville, WI 53547

Mini-Magic
(Ribbons and lace)
3910 Patricia Drive
Columbus, OH 43220
(614) 457-3687

Newark Dressmaker Supply
(Beads and pearls)
6473 Ruch Road
P.O. Box 20730
Lehigh Valley, PA 18002
(610) 837-7500

OK's Flowers, Inc.
(Freeze-dried flowers)
123 West 28th Street
New York, NY 10001
(212) 268-7231

Peking Handicraft
1388 San Mateo Avenue
San Francisco, CA 94080
(415) 626-8832

Perfect Packaging
(Paper favors)
1786 Bellmore Avenue
Bellmore, NY 11710-5522
(516) 783-3313

Rosie's Creations
New York, NY
(212) 362-6069

# Suggested Reading

Cole, Harriette. *Jumping the Broom: The African-American Wedding Planner.* New York: Henry Holt and Company, 1993.

Davis, Nancy. *Bridal Style: Concise Edition.* New York: Hugh Lauter Levin Associates, 1997.

Eisen, Armand. *The Wedding Book: A Bride's Memento.* Kansas City: Andrews and McNeel, 1992.

Ishee, Mark. *Wedding Toasts and Traditions.* Brentwood, Tenn.: JM Productions, 1986.

Jones, Leslie. *Happy Is the Bride the Sun Shines On: Wedding Beliefs, Customs, and Traditions.* Chicago: Contemporary Books, 1995.

Levin, Laurie and Laura Golden Bellotti. *Creative Weddings: An Up-To-Date Guide to Making Your Wedding As Unique As You Are.* Plume Books, 1994.

Long, Becky. *Something Old, Something New: A Bride's Guide: Creative Ways to Personalize Your Wedding.* Meadowbrook Books, 1998.

McBride-Mellinger, Maria. *Bridal Flowers: Arrangements for a Perfect Wedding.* Boston: Bulfinch Press, 1992.

———. *The Perfect Wedding.* New York: Collins Publishers, 1997.

McWilliams, Peter. *I Marry You Because . . .* North Hollywood, Calif.: Wilshire Publications, 1997.

Mullins, Kathy, and Andrea Feld, eds. *Bride's Little Book of Customs and Keepsakes.* New York: Clarkson Potter, 1994.

Nelson, Gertrud Mueller and Christopher Witt. *Sacred Threshold: Rituals and Readings for a Wedding With Spirit.* New York: Image Books, 1998.

Nitschke, Camela. *Holiday Ornaments I.* Video. Perrysburg, Ohio: Ribbonry, 1995.

Reekie, Jennie. *The London Ritz Book of Weddings.* New York: William Morrow and Company, 1992.

Rogers, Jennifer. *Tried and Trousseau: The Bride Guide.* New York: Fireside Books, 1992.

Smith, Jacqueline. *The Creative Wedding Idea Book: Bold Suggestions to Make Every Aspect of Your Wedding Special.* Bob Adams, Inc. Publishers, 1994.

Stewart, Arlene Hamilton. *A Bride's Book of Wedding Traditions.* The Hearst Corp., 1995.

Sturgis, Ingrid. *The Nubian Wedding Book: Words and Rituals to Celebrate and Plan an African-American Wedding.* Three Rivers Press, 1998.

Thomas, Pamela. *Bridal Guide: A Complete Guide on How to Plan Your Wedding.* Bridal Guide, 1994.

Van Der Meer, Antonia, ed. *Bride's New Ways to Wed: A Guide to Personalizing Your Wedding.* New York: Perigree Books, 1990.

# Index